T0246669

WE

CARRY

SMOKE

AND

PAPER

WE
CARRY
SMOKE
AND
PAPER

Essays on the

Grief and Hope

of Conversion

MELODY S. GEE

University of Iowa Press, Iowa City

University of Iowa Press, Iowa City 52242
Copyright © 2024 by Melody S. Gee
uipress.uiowa.edu
Printed in the United States of America

ISBN: 978-1-60938-975-8 (pbk)
ISBN: 978-1-60938-976-5 (ebk)

Cover design by Kathleen Lynch
Text design and typesetting by Ashley Muehlbauer

Printed on acid-free paper

Page vii, "Seamus Heaney, The Art of Poetry No. 75"
by "Seamus Heaney, The Art of Poetry No. 75,"
from an interview conducted by Henri Cole.
Copyright © 1997 by the Paris Review Foundation,
Inc, used by permission of The Wylie Agency LLC.

Catalog-in-Publication data is on file
at the Library of Congress.

FOR PAUL

I have begun to think of life as a series of ripples widening out from an original center. In a way, no matter how wide the circumference gets, no matter how far you have rippled out from the first point, that original pulse of your being is still traveling in you and through you. So although you can talk about this period of your life and that period of it, your first self and your last self are by no means distinct.

—SEAMUS HEANEY

CONTENTS

WE

CARRY

SMOKE

AND

PAPER

IDIOLECT

I say I grew up bilingual, but the truth is more about loss than duality. My earliest language was Taiwanese Mandarin, spoken by caregivers in the foster home outside Taipei, where I awaited adoption for the first nine months of my life. In the few pictures I have of that time, I am cared for by a woman who looks to be in her thirties, in a house full of other children, perhaps her own or other fosters. I sleep in a little cot with a woven bamboo mattress. My fluff of hair sticks straight up. And I am always dressed for warmth, bundled and jacketed even outside on sunny days. In the pictures where I am looking at someone beyond the camera, I try to imagine what words or sounds were holding my pose or eliciting my smile, what tones, if any, got imprinted on me, what traces may still remain.

When I arrived at my parents' home in California, Taiwanese Mandarin was replaced by my family's southern village dialect of Cantonese—my first language extinction. I grew up surrounded by second-language English speakers, recognizing Cantonese's lilting tones and clipped grammar forged into my family's English. I could predict exactly how my mom would ask one of our regular restaurant customers, "You want you same all the time order?" Though my dad was born in America, he grew up in an insular and isolated immigrant community, speaking Cantonese with more comfort and ease than English, and often with the same second-language markers as my mom.

Then, as for many children of immigrants, English displaced my parents' mother tongue when I started school. From age four, every new word I learned was in English, while with my parents and grandparents, I wore out the same few Cantonese phrases. "Ni haek-a meh?" (Have you eaten yet?) "Goi goi ho lah." (We are all doing well.) I never expanded my Cantonese vocabulary or learned to write more than the three characters in my name. With every English word I gained, a Cantonese one seemed to slip away. When I brought home new words, the outside world's currency, I hid them from my parents like a thief. I know they watched me grow my stash with confusion, fear, and an unmistakable flicker of relief. English was like an invasive species—multiplying, crowding out, devouring Cantonese with every nursery rhyme, television show, and new friend. I experienced the same loss that essayist Richard Rodriguez describes after he became fluent in English as a child: "Once I learned public language, it would never again be easy for me to hear intimate family voices."

Distant relatives or elders we ran into at the grocery store were incredulous when I answered in English, or when my labored and broken Cantonese could not carry me beyond a few weak responses to their questions. To them, fluency in our family language was a sign of respect for homeland, parents, and identity. But it was not for lack of filial piety that I was physically unable to untie my tongue. Mine was the same reason Rodriguez identifies as stripping him of his Spanish fluency: "A powerful guilt blocked my spoken words; an essential glue was missing whenever I'd try to connect words to form sentences. I would be unable to break a barrier of sound, to speak freely. I would speak, or try to speak, Spanish, and I would manage to utter halting, hiccupping sounds that betrayed my unease." The writer Amy Tan once described herself as speaking "a daughter's Shanghainese," able to speak, quite literally, only to her mother and only with words from a very young version of herself. I, too, could express myself only as a child: *hungry, tired, full, please.*

And yet, English did exactly what it was supposed to do: it gave me access and ability to navigate the world. English was my way of belonging to the country my parents believed would save their lives. Did they know being saved would come at such a price as their daughter, whose every sound, expectation, and feeling would require translation? What do we call an invasive species that the entire ecosystem will come to depend on?

—

When I started learning Spanish in high school, the grammar and the accent clicked in me, my tongue somehow agile in ways it no longer or perhaps never was with Cantonese. My friends and I got in a lot of conversation practice by talking clumsily about forbidden topics in front of our parents, or by talking about our parents right in front of them. After four years of study and countless episodes of *Destinos*, I started to describe myself as bilingual. Unlike Cantonese, I could use Spanish outside my home, and to talk about myself, my feelings, my experiences. Suddenly liberated from my lifelong shyness, I became eager to exchange pleasantries with strangers at the Mexican market where my grandfather bought meat for the restaurant. I took more classes in college and held simple but competent conversations with my freshman roommate's family every time she brought me home for her mother's pozole, which was always paired with a frosty bottle of orange Jarritos.

One afternoon during my sophomore year in college, as I rode the bus from campus to San Francisco, I helped a woman recently arrived from Mexico find her destination on the transit map and request the correct stop. I didn't notice my complete lack of resentment, which surfaced quickly whenever I was called upon to help my mom pump gas or ask whether a coupon could be doubled. I smiled at the woman on the bus and basked in the thrill of having a useful skill, while all my life my mom's needs had felt oppressive, like a tether keeping me ahead of her. My mom's English was actually pretty strong, but she lacked confidence in herself. When people spoke fast, she got flustered and frustrated. I wasn't there to translate so much as to catch and digest information, then offer her a slower, softer, less overwhelming version of what she'd heard, standing as a buffer between her and other people's idioms and impatience.

Whenever I resisted, embarrassed by my mom's requests, she would snap, "Just ask! It's so *easy* for you." It was, and yet when I spoke for her to clerks or attendants, my voice affected confidence while I felt exposed and anxious. I often wished my mom could show me how to make or get or do something, anything. I wanted for once to feel like she was in the lead, and I resented her for mistaking my fluent English for wisdom I didn't possess, and for needing me to never let on that I felt at sea, because then where would either of us be?

My daughters see their grandmother's talents—cooking, growing vegetables, sewing, speaking four dialects of Chinese plus English—and ask why I never learned these things from her. The answer is that I never asked. That she never offered or insisted, perhaps to avoid my sulking, perhaps because neither of us could ever quite navigate whether I was supposed to be her deferential daughter or assertive protector. So my mom cooked and sewed and gardened while I watched and absorbed a little from a distance, her American child, for whom she had fashioned and given everything out of the nothing she had arrived with.

One lesson in my first-year Spanish class haunted me: our words for things are arbitrary. My teacher, a Belgian immigrant, paced across the front of the room, pushing us in her French-studded English to see that names come from us and not the thing itself. "Is it *rock* or *piedra*? *Home* or *casa*? Which is the true name for the thing?" She swept her arms out, embracing us all with her point. "Your language," she insisted, "shapes how you see the world, but so does everyone else's. Allez! Get outside yourself and see that every language creates a different reality!"

I began to name things in my head, which was spinning in three languages. *Dog, perro, gao. Rice, arroz, faan.* Were none of them truly anchored to the world? Did my mom and I hear each other's English and Cantonese as not quite real? Neither she nor I had enough fluency to bridge our divide. The distance between me and my parents was an accretion of words, which, I had just learned, were all randomly assigned. Words themselves did not contain the essence of *daughter* or *nui*, for that would make one word less true than the other. Words could not measure the distance between my parents asking in one language and my answering in another.

My mom seemed agitated anytime she heard me speak Spanish, despite my ability to do things like bargain on her behalf with vendors at the Cypress swap meet. Once, after I made small talk with my parents' landscapers, she told me she didn't like the sound of Spanish, how ugly she thought its tones were. I laughed. To my ear, there was no harsher or more grating sound than everyday Cantonese. To listen to my mom and her best friend compare Hong Kong noodles found in Rowland Heights versus Monterey Park would be to easily mistake their fond reminiscences for bitter outrage and disgust. But my Spanish must have felt to her like utter betrayal and abandonment, a language I chose, which gave me to others while our silences stretched and strained.

About a year after I started learning Spanish, my mom began taking ESL classes at the local adult education center, to keep her mind sharp, she said. Perpetually anxious about aging, she was vigilant about bone loss, cholesterol, and dementia, which she treated with calcium pills, kumquat leaves, and now English classes. For an hour every morning before work at the restaurant, she identified parts of speech, grew a vocabulary list, and found new mah-jongg partners for the weekend. The only other time she had taken language classes was just after arriving in the United States at eighteen, though she only attended classes sporadically between grueling work in canneries and taking in sewing and mending jobs at night.

My mom struggled with the idioms and maddening irregularities of English. I had no answers for why the phrase *feather in your cap* meant an achievement you flaunt, or why we say *poke* after *slow* when urging someone to hurry up. As my daughters learned to speak in our family of native English speakers, they delightfully misapplied grammar rules like all children do: "The bad guy sworded the knight." "I jumped-ed in this puddle because my shoes are waterable." These early errors are evidence of innate grammar systems developing, and we find them enchanting, whereas we find second-language errors grating. My girls needed no correction. Their funny constructions disappeared naturally. They will not remember conjuring wholly new language from the depths of themselves, proving that one's mother tongue is not learned through imitation alone. But a second-language learner's errors, like my mom's inability to conjugate verbs, can seem impossible to surmount. I watched her repeat the same ESL homework year after year, unable to wrangle her tongue or her memory to overcome recurring errors, blanks, and broken connections, as she berated herself for lacking discipline and education. Linguists have called this fossilization, cessation of learning, or permanent failure. The names connote a hardening that blocks change or development. There's some debate about whether all learners, to some extent, are afflicted with this loss of flexibility, or if those who learn a second language outside their first language family, and those who begin learning later in life, are far more prone to it. Linguistic fossilization is a mystery precisely because it occurs despite motivation to learn, ample feedback, and opportunity to practice. For some learners, there seems to be a point beyond which they cannot advance. Whether or not her language acquisition was actually arrested, my mom certainly felt stalled and believed that her English was as good as it was ever going to be.

Or maybe it was less about inhibited pathways and more about avoiding further grief. Gaining a language is not a simple act of acquisition. The first stage of learning a new language is often called the silent period, necessary for the learner to absorb all the newness, and lasting sometimes for months. We have to lose our voice for a while, our tongues cocooned while our entire system of understanding ourselves and the world expands. During the silent period, we begin to comprehend before we can produce the new language, caging our intelligence and abilities behind the slow pace of our speaking skills.

Any language gain is also a negotiation. I learned the nuances among *feliz*, *contenta*, and *alegre*, which give new layers to *happy*. I learned the untranslatable *sobremesa*, the name for conversation savored at the table long after the meal is over, and my idea of a meal is forever altered. I also carry a primal dictionary of untranslatable Cantonese, like *hahm toi*, which names the smell of the clothes you've been wearing or the sheets you've been sleeping on. It means the particular smell of you, and it connotes familiarity along with others' revulsion. Hahm toi makes the world in English smell rather one-dimensional. Two languages require two systems to coexist and undergo continuous comparison. On the one hand, this enriches our senses. On the other, it requires endless shifting, balancing, and choosing just to make meaning. Sometimes, when my mom would lament, "My English is no good," it sounded more like she was saying, "English is not me."

A fossil seems like an immovable specimen locked forever in death. But a fossil is not actually a preserved bone. It's not bone at all. After a body's flesh has decomposed, bones usually disintegrate too. Only rarely does bone become trapped under enough earth or water, with pressure intense enough for minerals to seep into its cracks and pores and replace the living material with its deposits. What we discover after millennia is a rock replica of what had been femur, skull, pelvis—evidence and echo of life, but not life's actual remains. In the same way, I know my mom's English and my Cantonese are castings of former fluency, a former intimacy, which have shifted grain by grain, word by word. Even so, a fossil is not mere suspension of decay, nor is it simply a shadow or trace. It is release and replacement—of life, of language—in rare and perfect measure.

~

In 2015, my husband's teaching assignment brought us to his university's Madrid campus for the spring semester. Paul would teach his class and continue his departmental service, with long weekends free for us to explore the city or travel. We arrived in early February with our four-year-old and sixteen-month-old, breathless before the city's beauty, its pace and height, and its rapid-fire Spanish. Before our trip, my husband and I practiced diligently, ready to make our way in a new country and see all our years of language study pay off.

For good measure, I also studied maps of our corridor of the city, metro routes, museum hours, and restaurant menus.

After a blessedly smooth flight, we managed to get ourselves by taxi to our apartment, which we learned upon arrival wouldn't be available for another four hours. The super led us to a sparsely furnished studio on another floor. Paul and I muddled through the conversation, fairly certain we were just going to wait for our two-bedroom to be cleaned, and that the four of us had not suddenly been reassigned to a single room with a micro kitchen and doorless bathroom. Before we could settle in for a nap, the building manager came up to tell us that a portable crib for our younger daughter would be delivered to our apartment that evening, and then the rental stroller I had booked from home had arrived. I managed to complete both conversations without feeling entirely certain about what was being said or what exactly I was agreeing to. I kept saying "sí," "bueno," and "vale," though I was confused and unsure. I said the words as if to convince myself that I was fine with what was happening and that I still retained some agency. I was too embarrassed to ask the stroller agent to repeat what I couldn't catch, all my education and practice no match for the swallowed consonants and speed of Castilian Spanish. Like a child buying candy, I held out a palmful of euros and let the agent fish out our deposit.

At long last, we found ourselves unpacking in our correct and very lovely apartment. A corner two-bedroom unit on the fourth floor, it was fully furnished, even with a high chair, with one balcony off the living room and one off the bedroom, overlooking a traffic roundabout that churned day and night with taxis and buses. That first afternoon, Paul's American colleague dropped by to take us to lunch. Her warm Midwestern embrace and accent filled me with relief. She walked us down the block to a diner called VIPS (pronounced "veeps"), where our kids were handed coloring menus that offered burgers, chicken tenders, or spaghetti. Jet lag and homesickness made me tear up at the thoughtfulness of her choice, and we would return to this restaurant on many nights when we were too drained to coax them into paella. I asked Paul's colleague a few questions about the menu and prepared myself to order, but in the end, I just pointed at the pictures. We talked in English over the meal. Paul described the course he would teach. I told her that I was on leave from my teaching position and described our travel plans to Toledo, Ávila, Segovia, and Valencia. As I spoke them aloud, our ambitions suddenly felt foolish and out of reach, the idea of buying train tickets and booking hotels in Spanish now seemingly impossible after my first day's overwhelm at such straightforward tasks. As we ate, I was at once overcome with the desire to cling to this woman and never let her out of my sight, and to push her away so that we could prove ourselves on our own.

That first night after the girls went to bed, I retreated to our room and downloaded a candy game on my phone, swiping and crushing for what felt like hours of palliative wordlessness. I would do the same on many nights to come, my brain pounding a treadmill of the day's mistakes, omissions, and failures to understand. Back home, I had known and admired the immigrant parents of friends who demanded that America learn to understand their accents and pronounce their given names, standing firmly inside their right to be there and insisting their money was worth as much as anyone else's. I wanted to walk through Spain as they did in America. But instead, I cringed at my every mispronunciation. I fell silent, hoping for my gestures to convey enough and for my foreignness to disappear.

⁓

On our first Sunday in Madrid, we attended Mass at San Fermín de los Navarros, one of nine churches within a mile of our apartment. San Fermin was narrowly sandwiched between two seven-story apartment buildings, ribbed with Gothic arches and ornately pleated columns. As the gathering song began, I recognized the first notes of the choir's ethereal Latin "Ave Maria." During the presentation of the gifts, we heard the plaintive solo of "Gabriel's Oboe," my husband's favorite from the soundtrack of *The Mission*. I was transfixed by our first Mass in Madrid, but the cognitive strain—listening, translating, filling in the gaps I had missed while translating, then listening again—was depleting. Most of the liturgy sailed past me. Even the parts I caught were merely short relief, and I exited the church feeling like I hadn't actually been to Mass at all.

Less than two years into seeking within the Catholic Church, I was inside my own silent period, beginning to understand *grace, incarnation, worship, blessing,* but only on the cusp of expressing their meaning. Becoming a Catholic meant learning so many new words. Parts of the Mass: Introductory Rites, Liturgy of the Word, Liturgy of the Eucharist. Names of saints. The Nicene Creed that I and everyone else fumbled through reciting every Sunday. Consubstantiation turned bread and wine into the body and blood of Jesus. Church teachings are inscribed in a book called the catechism. I was gaining and revising words like this at every turn. Signs of holiness in our physical world: *sacramental.* The frigid feeling of God's complete absence or abandonment: *desolation.* "Consolation," my spiritual director said to me as I struggled to describe the warm and solid feeling of not pretending, posturing, or gossiping with a new friend. I looked back and inscribed *consolation* over old memories: my first pregnancy sonogram, discovering a new career after being laid off, walking across campus on my first day as a college freshman. As new words accrued, their meanings broadened me but also began to replace old ones, and the revisions unnerved me.

The language of faith, far from natural to me, was now mediated—more accurately, obscured—by a foreign language and my halting comprehension. I could not grow quiet in Madrid. I needed English to feel called, to hear God, to respond. The world in which I knew myself and shared myself in more than one language was gone. In a few days, Ash Wednesday would begin my second Lent as a seeker observing the rituals of fasting and receiving ashes on my forehead but not yet fully a member of the church. But this year, we gave ourselves a family dispensation from fasting and abstaining from meat. With the pressures of acclimation on us, the idea of giving up anything for the next forty days felt less like spiritual purification and more like torture.

In fact, everything began to feel like a battle. I couldn't relax, even in our snug apartment, even while just strolling to a late dinner with Paul while a sitter stayed with our sleeping girls. In the anxious vigilance I could not turn off, I felt my mom inside and all around me. I understood, profoundly, her anxiety and her attempts to manage it with endless tasks and monitoring of my dad and me. I understood her fear of new places, her constant worry that we would get lost, lose money, or get sick, and how her fears intensified in direct proportion to her linguistic discomfort. For the first time, I too felt my intelligence and the fullness of my whole self caged behind my lack of fluency. During much of our time in Madrid, my mind raced ahead to our return to the States in May. For almost sixty years in her adopted country, my mom has been holding the same desire for such relief.

For most of our time in Madrid, I was slow, tangled, and ungrounded. I felt defensive during the most benign interactions, which I spent hours overpreparing for, never certain that my vocabulary retrieval would be fast enough to get me through the task at hand. Easily overwhelmed, I pretended to understand far more than I did, then retreated into silence as soon as I could. The worst moments were in stores that didn't accept credit cards, forcing me to both apprehend prices correctly and then count out coins in Spanish. My mom always counted in Cantonese, and now I understood why. Nothing felt more unnatural than numbers and sums not in English. Actually, the worst moments were when my oldest threw tantrums whenever I held a conversation in Spanish for more than a few moments. Never given to outbursts at home, my usually easygoing four-year-old shrieked and flailed or bolted away as if possessed. How frightening it must have been to suddenly not understand what your own mother is saying.

When I looked at pictures from our time in Madrid, I realized that we had managed to buy groceries, eat out, hire sitters, hail taxis, and enroll the girls in classes. In truth, we had lived well and enjoyed extraordinary generosity and patience from others. Still, I felt lost and inadequate the whole semester, and ever so slightly unreal.

My weariness came from inhabiting a different version of myself, anxious for the real me to return once we landed back home. At the time, I didn't think of my mom, nor did I call her. What would she have made of me, crumpling from a day spent taking my girls to ballet and music, then dining in outdoor cafés with thirteen kinds of ham to choose from? Of my paralysis despite all my education, literacy, and translation apps? I could feel her inside the persistent agitation roiling in me.

Paul and I tried offering each other terms of endearment in Spanish. "Te amo" and "mi querida" sounded lovely, but also weightless against "I love you" and "sweetheart." When our little experiment failed, we retreated to "baby," the only word that called tenderly to our real selves, that endeared. I thought of how all my mom's words of care ("maan maan heak" for *eat slowly*) and anger ("ni moh yoong" for *you are useless*) came only in Cantonese. And so, her care and her anger, her superstitions and stories, all drifted on her side of our gulf, while all my words for desire and the future remained on mine. Each of our languages of intimacy was the other's language of limitation.

My body remembered other feelings before I did—an old tension, exertion, and blunt stubbornness with which I had moved through the world flooded me again. I had coped with my immigrant parents' dependency, how they needed me for things beyond my years and capability, by charging forward, half understanding, mostly guessing, and hoping for the best. I was around ten when they received bids for new kitchen flooring and asked me if I thought Pergo was the right material and who I thought would do the best job. While my friends went joyriding in their parents' beaters the morning of their sixteenth birthdays, I delayed applying for my learner's permit, predicting, correctly, that when I finally got my license at seventeen, my mom would hand over her Buick and ask me to take her everywhere. As children of immigrants themselves, my friends understood and gave me rides.

I faked my way through being my parents' guide to America. My confidence mimicked the adults around me. They were impressed, and I was terrified. My parents left me to deal with what they could not understand or navigate, with both profound trust in me and a need to shield themselves from the overwhelm and the unfamiliar procedures and language of SAT prep courses, college applications, financial aid seminars, or moving four hundred miles away to college. So my body long since knew how to push through and get close enough to good enough, and I shifted back into this gear in Spain. But when my hands shook as I bought metro tickets for a trip with two transfers, I fantasized about the older Spanish woman at the next kiosk gently taking my euros and doing it for me. Or for my daughter, all of four years old, to love me enough to take charge and relieve my panic.

Like my mom in the United States, I began to take a lot of pictures in Madrid. It was partly to capture evidence of the beauty and fun I knew I was missing all around me—but mostly so that I could sit with the images at the end of the day, just as my mom had done. I would use the pictures to tell myself the story of our day in English. In each image, I could experience the day without the strain of translation or being on guard, without having to live two steps ahead of the moment. I could see that our girls had delighted in the playgrounds and picnics, that they remained their exuberant and curious selves. Then, at last, the day I had just lived would feel like it had really happened to me and not like a stranger's dream I had white-knuckled my way through. I used to get so angry at my mom for missing every moment, for always getting lost in a crowd or falling behind because she was constantly taking pictures. But it was simply her way of living without her language, her only way to catch up to the life happening in words that did not match her reality.

Near the end of the semester, we sat on the patio of a tapas restaurant in a plaza of shops and cafés centered around a playground, where a parent could sit anywhere and have an eye on their kids while luxuriating in a crisp drink. Because our daughters were still used to eating dinner around five o'clock, which is too early to order a meal anywhere in Madrid, we would often order a dozen tiny tapas plates offered during the hour of merienda, when people were getting off work and looking for a beer and a bite and a quiet moment before heading home. The menu at this place was all idioms. One dish was called tigres (tigers). One was paja (hay). Another, matrimonio (marriage). This must be, I thought, what a Denny's or IHOP menu reads like to my mom, who found it infuriating to decipher food items where the description didn't square with its rhyming, alliterative, culturally coded name.

When our waiter arrived, Paul pointed to the menu and asked, "Qué es . . . matrimonio?"

The waiter put his pencil to his chin thoughtfully. "Ah," he replied, "es algo muy complejo y hermoso, si la pareja es la adecuada."

It took us a beat to metabolize the joke: "Ah, marriage is a very complex and beautiful thing, if the couple is right for each other," before Paul and I burst out laughing. The waiter smiled and explained that the appetizer was a pairing of two kinds of anchovies on toast. We passed on the dish and ordered our usual potatoes, ham, omelets, meat skewers, and fried cuttlefish, turning to each other with glowing satisfaction. We left the waiter an enormous tip, disregarding the culture of nominal tips for wait staff in Spain, who were all paid a living wage. We felt buoyant and suddenly sure we could live in this country forever. Until that moment, Spanish had been our rough instrument for survival, never spontaneous or light. Our first laughter had meant that, after months of inadequacy and agitation, another language could delight us after all.

⁓

A few weeks later, we packed our things and flew home. Stepping off the plane at JFK, I needed to find a bathroom before our next flight to St. Louis and began rehearsing how to ask in Spanish for the nearest one, only to realize that I didn't have to. I looked around at all the signs in English. I listened to a thick Queens accent on the loudspeaker. We were nearly home, just one English-speaking flight before returning to our lives. My body loosened a little, but my relief was shadowed by a sadness—that our time in Spain was over, that I would jump back into work and my daughter would start preschool, that our lovely dream of living abroad had ended so quickly. I started to forget all my anxieties and overwhelm, and the memory of Spain spun into one long and beautiful vacation.

At home again, the world fell back into place quickly. I navigated streets and stores without thinking. In control and unafraid, I could last-minute shop for dinner. I could pick up the phone without steeling myself. And yet, life seemed to have lost a dimension, a brightness, a presence. In Madrid, everything had been a negotiation—every word, thought, reaction, desire, even our very selves. We were not just living in a new city but, with every errand and transaction, battling to make our way. Of course, it had been exhausting, sometimes debilitatingly so, the constant learning and relearning, the grain of discomfort irritating every interaction. But when it was over, I felt like a spark had gone out. Partly, it was because we had fallen in love with the Spanish commitment to rest and leisure. No one in Madrid would think to eat lunch at their desk. No one would dream of skipping the siesta hour to power through their to-do list. But mostly it was that the negotiation of languages intensified everything—my concentration, my awareness, my senses. Interrogating meaning through a different language pinballed me between the foreign and the familiar, between myself and not myself. It's not that I learned to listen harder or longer. I had learned, finally, to relax enough to take in context and expression, to puzzle together everything beyond words that constitutes a language, including delight and surprise. At home, I missed feeling that suppleness of a sapling ready to bend toward wherever the sun shone.

There is a separate language that calls me to Mass, to prayer, and to the transcendent. It sounds both new and as native as any mother tongue. Learning this new language of mystery, sacredness, intimacy, gratitude, hope, and belonging, I struggle with fluency. I've uttered grief and estrangement with every word. As I acquire new terms, I find myself reframed, my understandings revised, and worried about what I am turning away from as I follow. But the word *convert* comes from the Latin *vertere*, meaning "to turn," and *con*, meaning "together." I am reminded that my turning is neither solitary nor partial, that what's being forged is an idiolect, not evaluated for correctness and not in conflict but negotiation with my whole self. I hope the language of faith, toward which I turn out of instinct or effort, does not rewrite me by erasure but by expansion, that it moves me, past and all, out and into everything. Not just as a new set of beliefs to take up, but as a desire to listen and learn to answer. It is the negotiation that makes the experience real and radiant.

In this way, my faith feels similar to my mom's English, created just as her new self was created: in this country and no other, under these circumstances and no others, for these reasons and for this life. Her English is not broken. It is both a string of errors and a thing unto itself. Every word carries an entire topography of experience and culture, tectonic plates of past and present colliding and reconfiguring with every expression. But there is no getting around it: my faith is another gulf my parents and I cannot swim or shout across. What raft will carry ashore *reconciliation* from our every shipwreck?

The poet Pádraig Ó Tuama notes, "God is given words in the first chapter of Genesis. The writers . . . considered that as among the first things God would be heard doing. Therefore, every possibility of a person putting words to something, especially something difficult, in itself is a sacrament." For now, the language of faith comes to me through English, but I hold to the possibility that I will not have to choose one sacramental language from among the one extinguished in infancy, the one that cleaves me, however unsteadily, to my family, the one that feels most real but anchors me to the world outside them, or the one I learned as respite from all the others. Faith is believing that the next time words don't match my expectations, I may be caught off guard by the grace of astonishment instead of fear, that future matrimonio moments will deliver awe. I hope. Espero. Ngoi hei mong.

CHINESE AMERICAN

"I talk, you listen," my mom began. It was November 2005, and I expected something about Thanksgiving plans. I took the phone from the crook of my shoulder and put it against my ear. My mom's news has always come to me like this. In Cantonese, "I talk, you listen" is the literal translation of "ngoi gong ni heng," which can mean "listen up"; "I have something to tell you"; or "I told you so."

"What is it?" I asked in English.

She replied, in English, "Ah-Yeh is in the hospital."

"What happened?"

She switched back to Cantonese. "He fell in his bathroom last night. He laid there all night until Uncle Terry came in the morning."

My grandfather lived in the apartment above our family's restaurant. I wasn't alarmed at my mom's news at first; my grandfather had taken several falls in the past few years as his muscles weakened and his bones thinned. He would bruise himself, sometimes badly, and endure short hospital stays.

"How is he?"

"He hurt his head and his back. Your Uncle Terry is waiting at the hospital now."

After my grandmother died in 1990, my grandfather began his retreat. First, he stopped cooking and would only descend the two flights of stairs from his apartment to sit amid the din of the restaurant, chopping vegetables and trimming meats. Sitting on a high stool for leverage and gravity, he managed to do several hours of prep work each day. Arthritis had just begun arching his back and sculpting his hands into unusable claws. Within a few years, he was staying in the apartment all day, shuffling around with the help of a walker and metal railings we installed. First, we moved his radio, then his TV, and finally his recliner from the living room to his cramped bedroom, so that by the time he fell, sixteen years after my grandmother's death, he was spending every waking and sleeping hour in that rocker. He watched National League baseball in the summer and Caribbean League in the winter from the patchy brown chair he never rocked. My mom or uncle brought up his meals on covered trays and later retrieved the scraps and bones.

In the restaurant below him, work had gone on. My mom, my dad's brother, Uncle Terry, Terry's wife, Auntie Betty, and sometimes a cousin during the Saturday dinner rush, churned out hot cartons of food for patrons all over Los Angeles. The restaurant that for so long *was* my grandfather became a thing of its own without him, and my mom, aunt, and uncle inherited its work.

"What are you going to do?" I asked my mom. I meant the question more for myself. I was living in Indiana and teaching as an adjunct at the university where Paul was getting his doctorate. I didn't think I could afford to fly back to see my grandfather in the hospital. I wasn't sure I could if he died.

"What do you mean, 'do'?" my mom asked in English.

"I mean, will you close the restaurant?"

I don't know why I asked. We all knew we would never close the restaurant as long as my grandfather was alive. Even as it declined, was moribund, really, for the last few years, everyone knew closing it would kill him faster than his failing heart. But my mom answered without pause.

"Maybe. Maybe, yes."

—

My father's parents opened their first restaurant in Hollywood in the early 1950s. It failed within a year. Next, they bought into a place in Chinatown with two partners, but infighting forced them to sell their share. On their own with four school-aged children, my grandparents picked a site in Bellflower, near a busy freeway and amid new car dealerships and apartment buildings, with hopes that hungry salesmen and families would help start up their new business, Jack's Kitchen, named for my grandfather. Other restaurants contained some combination of a few standard words: *lucky, dragon, wok, emperor, panda, star, happiness.* Using my grandfather's American name and picking a location away from any Chinese community seemed to signal striking out on his own.

My grandparents poured the last of their savings into blue paint, new appliances, and a six-foot sign glowing in the middle of Lakewood Boulevard. For the first months, sales were miserable. My grandparents filled a dumpster with all the unsold food they couldn't eat themselves. Every day, my grandmother took two buses into Chinatown, where she found seamstress work to pay some of the restaurant's expenses. On her way, she left stacks of menus on benches and bus seats and made my dad and his siblings stick menus under doormats and windshield wipers everywhere they went. Slowly, customers started coming, then coming back for more.

Since 1956, many used car dealers have come and gone in the lot next door. A flower shop across the street was razed to make room for a motel and its parking lot. Henry Moffett's chicken pie restaurant moved out to Arcadia. Somehow, Jack's Kitchen managed to stay open despite the city changing all around, and managed to change very little itself. My grandparents' menu never varied from the day they opened. Customers who had been coming in since they were children cherished the familiarity and said the restaurant was the only place from their childhood that remained untouched. One customer remembered driving twenty miles with his dad from Garden Grove to pick up No. 3 combination dinners and extra egg rolls. They all remembered my father before he was married, my mom when she first arrived from Sacramento, twenty years old and untrained, shy but smiling. She had worked in canneries and sewing factories before they married, but nothing had prepared her for a new life away from her own mother, as a wife, cook, and daughter-in-law.

What I remember: Uncle Terry's radio that only picked up AM, and the wood-facade RCA television with a rabbit ears antenna. My cousins' red bean and egg custard tarts hidden behind the bell peppers in the last refrigerator. Rows of white take-out containers lining the wall by the giant rice warmer, buckets of vinegar, pineapple juice, and red food dye for making sweet and sour sauce. My mom and aunt eating lunch every day on the same faded dishes from a Chinatown discount stand. Their meals were simple and never fried, with more pungent flavors of salt-cured fish, fermented black beans, ginger, and bitter melon. The backyard overgrown with failed attempts to cultivate a squash patch, and the stumps of plum and persimmon saplings that refused to flower.

Until I started high school, I spent every afternoon at our restaurant. Every time I walked through the rusted security door, the air hit me hard—the heavy oil and salt, hissing fan blades, and metal spatulas clanging the woks. After school, I dropped my bag at the door and sat at the counter to take phone orders from our American customers. I shouted over the rumbling fans, and I absorbed the smell of deep-fat frying meats and dark soy sauce. Almost no one left tips at a take-out place, but sometimes, if I carried an order down the front steps and into their car, some would let me keep their change. I stashed these coins to buy M&Ms from friends raising money for their soccer teams. Saturday nights we stayed late to soap and scrub every inch of concrete floor and cooking surfaces, our hands puckering from the caustic detergent and scalding water.

By the time I came along, my cousins were in high school. The children of my dad's brother and sister were more than ten years older than me and had grown up in the restaurant together. I envied them their companionship and the way they seemed at home in the restaurant, helping themselves to leftover fried shrimp, a can of fruit cocktail, or a soda whenever they liked, dancing around my mom and aunt at the woks to grill themselves a hamburger. The oldest four had helped haul groceries from Chinatown, stuff and fold dumplings, answer the phone, and work the register. The cousin closest to my age was three years older, but he was usually tagging along with his siblings or spending his days with kids in the neighborhood behind the restaurant, whose houses my mom decided were too far for me to venture to. When I was very young, my older cousins came and went with their friends and each other, sometimes stopping to play a quick card game or watch television with me while inhaling a dish their mom or mine had prepared, always taking the leftovers home. Sometimes they would drop off a stack of *LIFE* magazines for me to flip through. But they went off to college and work, and I spent most of my time in the restaurant among the adults, trying to find a comfortable place to hide away from the clamor.

The restaurant walls were fourteen feet high, but they could not always keep out strangers. Even though we installed steel accordion gates across the front windows and glass doors, already a constellation of stray bullets, thieves broke in through the back and knocked over the register in vain, looking for the cash we carried upstairs each night. Once they came in and took nothing but overturned buckets of soy sauce and smashed cans of tomato paste across the walls. Another time they broke into the storage unit and stole dozens of whole chickens from our chest freezers.

Several times a year, our restaurant endured health inspections—surprise afternoon visits from inspectors who were often themselves immigrants from China, the Philippines, or Indonesia. Sometimes, if the inspector wanted to get done quickly, or if he was from our region of Guangdong and sympathetic, he would call ahead. "Wei sahng!" my mom or aunt would cry out, slamming down the phone and rushing to straighten what they could before the inspector arrived with his clipboard.

We usually got through inspections silently, watching doors get opened, sauces scrutinized, vegetables prodded. They checked refrigerator temperatures, the proximity of raw meat to vegetables, made-on dates, and cooking surfaces, ready to choose between a bright blue A slip, a green B, or a red C to post in the front window. They inspected our bathroom and our backyard. In the walk-in pantry, where I usually maintained a nest of *TV Guides*, homework, candy, and scrap paper, they poked my things with their feet and decided it wasn't hazardous to the dried goods.

When I was in sixth grade, an inspector we didn't know arrived unannounced late one afternoon. He was a small man in a gray, wrinkled city uniform. He wasn't white, but we couldn't place his accent or guess where he was from. Since no customers were around and the phone wasn't ringing, both Auntie Betty and my mom followed him, trying to make polite talk.

The inspector was quiet and officious, moving swiftly through his checklist with narrowed eyes, clicking and unclicking his pen. He opened two freezers in the prep area and stopped.

"Where's the date on these?" he asked, pointing with his pen at several plastic tubs stacked high with pyramids of battered and flash-fried egg rolls, waiting for their final bath in scalding lard before being tucked into a waiting order. The strips of masking tape each tub displayed on its front were worn, and the dates all rubbed out.

"All made within one week," Auntie Betty assured him. "Everything fresh."

The inspector turned one tub a quarter turn and examined the food from another angle.

"No," he said, shaking his head.

"Yes," my mom insisted. "Yes, we make egg rolls every Sunday. So, today is Thursday. Not even one week old." She looked to Auntie Betty for a supportive nod.

The inspector replied, "Well, you don't have a date on them, so how do I know they're fresh? Why should I believe you? You could say anything."

"We tell you they are," my mom said quietly, her eyes never raised above his tie. "We are clean."

He clicked his pen and shoved it in his front pocket. "Listen, no date, no egg rolls."

He moved quickly. Within a few seconds, each tub was drawn from its shelf, and dozens of egg rolls were emptied into the garbage. He told my mom to find him a bottle of bleach.

"What for?" she asked.

"I know how you work," he said. "I know you'll just take food straight out of the garbage after I leave. Well, not this time."

My mom handed him the bleach. Pouring in rhythmic circles, he drained the entire bottle onto the egg rolls. Their soft, yellow skins sizzled and then turned pale green. Satisfied, he dropped the empty bottle on top of the ruined food.

"Now, get rid of that trash can, too," he said. "You can't have bleach in the food area."

The air smelled different after an outsider had been in the back. We felt invaded. My mom and aunt seethed for days about the health inspector, the bleach, and the B rating he gave us, but nothing ever got reported, not to the health department or the police.

We spent almost all our time at the restaurant. We didn't have a community of unrelated aunties and uncles because my parents didn't have time to socialize. And anyway, the restaurant made us loud and brusque and awkward. We either kept our distance or we yelled. We didn't know how to mingle or make small talk, how to have anyone over for dinner—we didn't even visit each other even though my dad and all three of his siblings lived in the same city. Maybe if there had been other people, being Chinese would have felt more expansive, more inclusive, less isolating and backbreaking. Chinese was not an ethnic identity so much as a synonym for *family*, and ours belonged inside the restaurant.

As a child, I called myself Chinese because my parents and grandparents were Chinese. Every kid in my school did the same, claiming our immigrant parents' homeland as our identity because citizenship in our families was at stake. I already answered them in English and refused their food in my lunch box. I spoke fast around my friends so that my mom had no hope of catching our conversation or joining in. And yet I couldn't say that I was not from the same place as my parents. Where would any of us belong then? If nowhere feels like home, we could only belong to each other.

⁓

A few months after my grandfather's fall, I came home for a visit during my university's winter break. I went with my parents to visit him in the recovery center where he had been since his fall. He had shown little improvement since arriving, refusing to exercise and snapping at physical therapists who cycled his legs and pumped his arms. He had also, very early in his stay, stopped eating. The center sent my grandfather to a psychiatrist, who asked to meet with my parents.

"Huh," my mom said to me as we navigated the hallways toward my grandfather's room. "This doctor tried to tell us Grandpa is *depressed*. He says we have to put him on medication for being *depressed*." She hissed the last word. "Gong muat gui, ah? Kai-ai!"

The rhetorical question is roughly translated as, "What in the hell are you talking about?" The epithet, however, I cannot translate. My cousin and I tested it out frequently when our moms were out of earshot. It meant something like *jerk* or even *asshole*, but we didn't know for sure. Eventually, an afternoon filled with "Hey, kai-ai, give me the remote" so deflated the insult that we grew tired of it. Our restaurant's volatile neighbor, Richard, who threw his garbage into our yard and told people waiting in line that we kept dead cats in the freezer, was a kai-ai. So was every health inspector and every faceless vandal who smashed in our windows or bubble-lettered graffiti on our building. But so was my Uncle Terry when he screwed up an order, so I wondered how bad it could be.

"The doctor doesn't know," my mom continued, "that old people say this all the time. This is how you make your children show respect for their parents. A good son says, 'Don't die—live for us.' This is how we talk!"

The idea of emotions debilitating your ability to work was beyond my family's comprehension. Feelings were to be overpowered by strenuous labor and sacrifice, or discarded as shameful if they got in the way of your productivity. My mom's frustration was compounded by her discovery that my grandfather wasn't eating simply because he didn't like the food. Trying to tempt him one day with savory melon soup and dumplings, perhaps somewhat afraid that he actually was depressed, my mom soon found out that he was perfectly willing and able to eat, just not the facility's salt-free vegetables and meatloaf. Now, someone was cooking and delivering food to him three, sometimes four times a day.

As we approached my grandfather's open door, my mom whispered, "Don't say anything about the restaurant or he'll ask if we're busy."

I suddenly realized that it was the middle of the afternoon, right before the dinner rush would begin.

"Wait, is the restaurant closed?" I asked.

"We only open for a few hours a day now, but don't say anything."

"I won't," I promised.

I saw my grandfather's feet sticking out beyond the half-drawn curtain around his bed. His neighbor was completely enclosed behind his own two curtains.

"Hi, Grandpa," I said, shuffling against his bed rail. The hospital gown made him look jaundiced and small.

"Mm," he nodded, closing his eyes and jutting out his chin as he always did when greeted.

"Ni ho mah? Heak faan mayuh?" (Are you well? Have you eaten yet?)

"Mm," he answered.

The recovery center reminded me of my grandmother's nursing home, where she had lived for several years after a brain tumor operation left her in a vegetative state. This place's bleached stench, the abandonment, and the terrible cheerfulness of the staff were all too familiar. Behind me, a physical therapist in pink scrubs suddenly appeared and abruptly pulled back the curtain. She told my grandfather it was time for his therapy in the workout room.

"No. Leave me," he moaned and batted her away.

"Yes, we have to exercise," she said with a lilting impatience.

"Take me home," my grandfather said. He pointed at us. "Take me out of here."

Both my parents assured him that we would as soon as he finished his therapy and could walk on his own.

"Okay, okay," he relented, but still didn't get up. "Exercise tomorrow, okay?"

The therapist said, "No, Mr. Gee, today."

With all our arms braced around him, we got my grandfather to sit up and swing his legs over the side of the bed. He panted hard, his chest heaving and arms shaking. I didn't know how often he was actually doing his therapy, but he had barely enough strength to hold his head up.

"Gah," he sputtered, still clutching at someone's two arms near him. "Gah!" He leaned over, and I could see the peaks of his spine and the veins on his back through the loosely tied gown. "Gah . . . Goddamn it!"

We all eased our grips. My grandfather's arms went limp at his side, and he continued moaning and heaving.

"Okay, okay," he whispered finally. He reached up for our arms again and quieted. "If I do this, I go home?"

"Yes," we all assured him.

"Oh, I want to die! Why don't you all just let me die?"

"No, no! No one wants you to die. We want you to live for us."

We finally left him in the crowded and sunny workout room, as the therapist wheeled him between low parallel bars that he could barely wrap his fingers around.

"Tomorrow," he said, holding the bars weakly. "Come take me home tomorrow."

"Okay," we called back.

⁓

"When the restaurant closes and I have time," my mom often said of the many things she wanted to do—trips she wanted to take, time to shop, sew, and garden—if only she were not cooking. I wanted these things for her, too. Yet I could not conceive of us without the restaurant, our days and routines so tightly defined by its running. My mom knew nothing about restaurant work when she married my father but was expected to learn quickly over long, exhausting days. Though the restaurant was my dad's to inherit, it was my mom who developed all the cooking skills and business sense. My dad grew up helping in the restaurant, and it took him ten years to finish college between all the demands of daily supply runs to Chinatown or constant equipment repairs. He began programming computers in the 1980s, and the list of clients who needed custom databases grew quickly. With well-paying office work to support his family, my grandparents didn't expect my dad to run the restaurant. He had never actually learned to cook in all those years anyway. But there was never a question that *someone* would have to help run the restaurant. My mom knew on her wedding day that this would be her life's work, her service to her in-laws, and the price of joining this family who were making it on their own in America. My Auntie Betty knew the same when she married my dad's brother.

In the early days, my mom didn't sleep much. She spent mornings cooking the day's rice, pinching together won tons and sui mai, mixing egg foo young batter, thickening vats of gravy, and filling deep bins with diced vegetables and marinated meats. She did the first deep fry for egg rolls, butterflied shrimp, and sweet and sour pork chunks. In the evening, my mom peeled away the old socks she altered into protective sleeves, revealing burns down her arms from oil spatters, boiling water, and hot utensils. She pricked her blisters with a safety pin and smeared her hot, rippled skin with pungent Ching Wan Hung cream. On the tops of her feet and the rest of her aching muscles, she dabbed White Flower Oil, lacing the air with camphor, eucalyptus, and menthol.

The restaurant opened at four o'clock, and every component for every meal needed to be ready because, until closing at nine o'clock, there was no rest between cooking, boxing, and serving food. When I was small, I stayed out of the way, in the back or upstairs in my grandparents' apartment, but when I was old enough to be helpful, I monitored the phone and the register. Slowly weekdays grew less busy, then the weekends too. By the time I was in junior high, we opened from noon to nine, hoping to capture more customers as each year we made less and saw fewer regulars. Often my mom and Auntie Betty were left with long, empty afternoons that even the food prep and cleaning couldn't fill.

I stopped going to the restaurant just as I started high school. I needed to stay home, I said, where there was a computer, all my books, and quiet for studying. I knew my parents would prioritize good grades over dinner rush help. And my grades really were slipping. I had always gone to bed well past eleven o'clock, after we were all home and showered. By middle school, I could no longer handle the sleep deprivation. Mornings were just the beginning of my all-day fight against my body's ache for more rest. I was zoning out in class, earning low Bs, which seemed to my parents far below what any good college would accept. I could stay home, they said. The customers could wait a few more rings on the phone. My mom and aunt could make do with their English.

What was also true was that I wanted to watch cable and talk to my friends instead of taking phone orders all afternoon in the sweltering heat, with only *I Love Lucy* or *COPS* on in the background. That first Saturday I stayed home alone, I lay on my bed and talked on the phone for five hours. I blew off my homework and my mom's chicken and rice, and I ate Cheetos and instant ramen and watched *Star Trek*, *The X-Files*, and *The Simpsons* until my parents came home at ten thirty. I didn't miss the restaurant noise or the constant errands. Or feeling lonely amid my family's chaos, exhaustion, irritability, and resignation.

Many nights my mom would tell me the day's total was less than four hundred dollars, compared to the peak years when they would make ten times that amount in one evening. I was barely beginning to understand that the restaurant would not stay open forever, that its purpose would be served when all the grandkids could support themselves with better-paying and less punishing work. No one taught us anything about the business or about cooking. No one repainted the sun-bleached walls or replaced aging appliances because none of it would be passed on. This was a life raft, not a legacy. But none of us knew how to let the restaurant die a good death. Or how to live without survivor's guilt. So we lamented its decline and lived in the shadow of former success, never considering whether we'd actually been happier when the lines snaked around the block. All we knew was to say, "Don't die. We want you to live for us," with reverence and honor and stubborn cleaving.

At home, I had hours to myself after school and all weekend. My dad worked in his home office, and I stayed in my room, studying or not. Sometimes we ate leftovers together; sometimes we took dinner to our rooms. I savored the quiet and privacy, even as I knew how much work was happening at the restaurant while I basked in air conditioning and free time. For the first time, I could join activities and friends. I played JV volleyball very briefly before finding a better fit on the yearbook staff and in art classes. I cheered on friends in school plays and talent shows and went along for milkshakes afterward. My world expanded, and everything, instantly, felt vast and possible. And none of it was scary. People could be trusted to keep me safe, even to feed me and get me home. Most of all, they talked to me. I spent afternoons at friends' houses and stayed for dinner, sometimes helping to cook or wash up. I discovered I loved burgers with everything on them, kimchi, dolma, and Alfredo sauce. My friends' families didn't eat with the television on. They told rounds of knock-knock jokes, debated whether art school is as good an investment as traditional college, and analyzed LA sports and local politics, while my friends' dads blasted Led Zeppelin, Three Dog Night, Cream, and the Allman Brothers Band. I also learned to eat slowly, to look up from my food, and to leave breath between bites for conversation. I got asked out and went to dances. I found everything thrilling, as if I'd arrived in a new country but with a secret fluency I'd always possessed. I belonged out here with more ease than I had ever imagined.

Many nights, I went to bed before my mom came home. Sleep was glorious and plentiful now. On the weekends, I usually slept past the time she left for the restaurant, which felt ever further away. Some summer mornings, after I got my license, I drove my mom across two freeways and down the pulsing artery of Lakewood Boulevard to drop her off at work. I always walked her in and waited for her to change her shoes, tie up her apron, and cinch her hair net. Nothing in the restaurant ever looked different or out of place. Sometimes she packed a few leftovers or ripe fruit for me to take home. I always thanked her and hurried away from the heavy air and piercing guilt. She never asked me to stay and help. If I offered to come on a busy day, she brushed me off and told me to study, even if it was Labor Day or the Fourth of July. A few of my cousins still came over on an occasional Friday or Saturday night, slipping comfortably into aprons and paper hats to help fill orders and deep clean. They had all known the restaurant for much longer than I had, through its best and busiest days. Maybe they didn't need to be asked to help. Maybe when they left, their mothers couldn't detect such obvious relief in their eyes.

Strangely enough, I learned to cook at home. The Food Network was becoming popular, and I watched chefs and regular people, none of them Chinese, prepare food in beautiful kitchens, plating and garnishing with care. On TV, a meal could be an affair of smiling, warm lighting, and pleasure. I watched, transfixed, as meat turned silken during an hours-long braise, as starchy pasta water helped emulsify a sauce. And the episodes didn't end when the food was cooked. Hosts sat down to the meals they had just prepared with their camera-ready friends and family. I realized I had picked up a lot about cooking from watching my mom, everything learned without words. I knew to add sugar to every sauce, that cornstarch slurries don't fully activate until the sauce reaches a full boil, and that rice needed to be washed and then covered with water one knuckle high to cook properly. But for my mom, all cooking was a labor, an endless preparation of the same five take-out dishes she herself did not want to eat. At home, on her one day off a week, she made simple meals of steamed fish, Chinese sausages, and dark greens. She substituted with frozen vegetable medley or kielbasa if that's what we had on hand, shooing me away when I offered to help because I slowed her down. We ate and washed up quickly, like at the restaurant.

The recipes I attempted tried my mom's patience. Too many steps or too much prep time drove her crazy, and nothing I cooked could be considered efficient. Once I stocked the fridge with canned crescent rolls and several large apples to be sliced and simmered in butter and sugar for a breakfast pastry the next morning. My mom, up early as always, glanced at the recipe on the counter, then minced my apples, unpeeled, and microwaved them to speed up the process. When I woke up crestfallen instead of grateful, she took offense and left for work early.

I made platters of slow-cooked meats and root vegetables, creamy pastas, and casseroles, none of which my mom's Chinese palate could tolerate. She did not do dairy, bread, tomato-based sauces, desserts, raw vegetables, or anything oven-roasted and served in heaps out of a single baking dish. For her, meals required several small plates of bite-sized, soy sauce–based vegetables and trimmed meats, centered around a bowl of rice. She wanted dishes that were separate and precise, not indiscernible lumps. Her expectations of filial piety evaporated like a quick deglaze, with a daughter who could cook but not for her mother. I ate my own leftovers for days on end.

In a few years, I would go to college four hundred miles away. I would stop calling myself Chinese long before then. On the UC Berkeley campus, away from my small high school where we identified with our parents' countries of origin, no one saw me as Chinese. I felt part of something else now—a generation of immigrants' kids trying to be successful Americans for our families but not so successful that we become foreign to them. I met others holding all the same tensions—competing cultural expectations, acceptable behaviors, desires, ambitions, identities, and loyalties.

Saying I was Chinese was no longer about closeness with my family, if it ever was. It had always been more of a way to say that I belonged with their feeling of not belonging here. But I wanted to and did belong to America with all its risks, pains, and delights. I could face it all with English and cultural literacy, which my family did not know whether to celebrate or mourn.

When I came home during college breaks, I didn't go to the restaurant except to drop off or pick up my mom. Sometimes I carried sliced pears or a thermos of tea upstairs to my grandfather. Other times, my mom said it was too late to bother him. I hadn't known that asking to stay home and study would mean the end of my time at the restaurant, of the hours alongside my mom, aunt, and the slowing stream of customers. My life had become my grandparents' dream, filled with education, work, travel, love—with opportunities. Like it did for everyone, what was home to me as a child became "my parents' house." And the restaurant went from being "our restaurant" to "my mom's work."

―

I saw my mom at her mother's funeral in Sacramento, three months after my brief visit to my grandfather's nursing home. Somewhere in the blur of the service, she told me they had set a date in July to close the restaurant. There was no reason to go on. No one believed my grandfather was coming home. He had quit physical therapy altogether. He ate some, but not much, of what was cooked and brought to him every day. My parents filled his room with things from home, trying to make it a little warmer, but he hardly looked at the pictures or watched anything on his little television. He hardly moved. My parents and aunt and uncle visited diligently, but there was little to say, and the visits were frequent but short. He never asked how the restaurant was doing.

"Why wait until July?" I asked.

"We have to make plans," she explained.

They would sell off whatever utensils and equipment they could, give whatever frozen meats and canned goods they had to neighbors, and toss the rest. They put up signs in English to tell customers these would be the last months.

"What are you going to do after?"

"Oh, maybe something. An office job, or maybe take some classes. I don't know yet," she mused. I was happy for her.

In July, the building was locked up. No one was interested in buying it, not even as a tear-down. My parents and aunt and uncle had emptied it out as best they could. I knew my mom would have noticed how quiet it was with the fans off. How vast it must have seemed with the shelves pulled from the walls. I thought of that air, thick and oily and unmoving, layering over the dust until the whole building, its cement floors, six dented wok burners, and opaque windows were all petrified to a slick, solid stillness.

By the end of August, my grandfather was dead.

I arrived at my parents' house on a Saturday, the night before the funeral. The semester had just started, and students in the four classes I was teaching had all just submitted essay drafts, which I had lugged across two time zones. My now-husband, to whom I would be engaged by the end of that year, was living on a grad student stipend and had just started all of his classes as well. I insisted that I would go by myself. He asked again and again if I was sure. I told him not to worry. In truth, my mom had also told me, "When you're married, then he comes," as if I hadn't yet earned my plus one.

During dinner in my parents' kitchen, the funeral home called to say that no one had been able to find a tie among my grandfather's things. They needed one that night to dress the body. My dad had suggested bringing over one of his own, but my mom cried out that it would be the worst luck and sent him out to buy one.

"Red?" my dad had asked, presuming the color of luck and prosperity would be a good choice.

"No!" my mom said in horror. "Not red!" But she said nothing more. My dad left for the mall, mystified.

My mom and I spent the rest of that evening stuffing quarters and Werther's candies into little red envelopes to press into the palms of mourners the next day. As I was hanging up my funeral clothes in my childhood bedroom, my mom came in and asked me to write something down for her. It was a eulogy that the funeral home's minister would read at the service. I listened and took notes as my mom told me what details of my grandfather's life she knew, how my grandfather came to America alone when he was a boy and worked his way up through multiple Chinatown kitchens, from washing dishes and emptying lard trays to being a full cook. She used words like *hero* and *deeply revered*, and told me to type it all up in big letters.

I was exhausted, and my mind was on the seventy papers sitting in my suitcase, my uninvited boyfriend who I wished were there, and the rest of my world that felt so far away from the restaurant and my parents' home. I rushed together a choppy, unpolished life story in overly simple language for a stranger to read.

Rose Hills is a sprawling memorial park in Whittier, California, all rolling and winding roads and rather steep grave sites. The grave markers are all granite rectangles embedded in the grass so that you can't read the name until you are standing right above it, and you need a map to direct you to the correct gate, section, lot, and grave number. My grandmother was buried here in 1990, and my grandfather's reserved plot next to hers had been carefully avoided every time we visited. I was nine when my grandmother died, and no one spoke to me about her death or at her funeral. I remember a limo picking us up in front of the restaurant. I remember my mom scolding me for being excited about it. Beyond that scrap, our silence seems to have prevented anything more from forming into memory. I remember that right after my grandmother's funeral, I popped in Johnny Cash's mournful album *Silver*, which sat among a dusty pile of tapes my dad bulk ordered from a catalog, the same way he ordered books, magazines, rocks, gems, and tools he never touched. I remember the moment my dad strode over to my boom box and snapped off the music with an abrupt, "No more. Too sad." Apart from that, my parents have not talked about my grandmother or her death since.

My grandfather's casket was open and waiting for us at the front of the chapel, flanked on both sides by floral stands and arrangements. Some were draped with silk sashes covered in Chinese characters. The chapel was airy and modern, with church-like stained glass and a movable altar for easy transformation. Maybe it was the makeup or the filtered light or the casket lining in pale cream silk that made my grandfather's face and hands look gray and chalky. He was laid out in a black suit and my dad's pick of a gray and white tie. Propped on an easel by the casket was his portrait, softly blurred and technicolored in the style of the 1940s. The over-the-shoulder headshot showed a slender, serious face, long before jowls set in deeply, before hair silvered and thinned. He had been six feet tall, a giant among his peers in Chinatown. I hadn't seen him stand up in over ten years.

My mom told me that when she and my dad were visiting him the day he died, my grandfather had been agitated. Out of nowhere, he insisted on getting up and walking on his own. Weak from months in bed, he couldn't even turn on his side without help. The realization of his own body's failure seemed to sink in, and he began to wail. Then he was shouting in pain as his heart gave out.

"He saw us last," my mom told me. "Not strangers."

Everyone, family or not, bowed three times before the casket when they entered. The immediate family members lit three sticks of incense, bowed again, then planted the incense in porcelain canisters filled with sand so the smoke continued to rise and curl. My cousins and I took our places in the pews behind our parents, and I turned back to see the seats filled with relatives and acquaintances I didn't know. When all the mourners finally arrived and filled the chapel, the Rose Hills minister, whom we were meeting for the first time, handed out bolts of cloth to my dad and his three siblings, whispering instructions to each. We watched my dad take his turn first. He walked stiffly up to the casket and laid his gray cloth on my grandfather's chest, tucking it around his arms. I wondered if the body felt stiff or cold. Then my Uncle Terry laid his down, a little lower to make sure my dad's cloth was still showing.

"What are those for?" I whispered to my mom as my dad's sister and youngest brother walked up with their dark cloths in hand.

"Oldest son's cloth goes closest to father's heart," she answered.

"Yes, but why are we laying the cloth on him?" I asked.

"Tradition."

My Auntie Elsa and Uncle Victor both bowed before returning to their seats, which my dad and Uncle Terry had not done. Minutes before the service was to start, my mom tapped me on the shoulder and held out a piece of paper.

"I need you to do me a favor," she said.

"What?"

My mom squeezed in next to me and handed me the eulogy I had typed and printed.

"I need you to read this," she said.

"Why, is there a mistake?"

"No. I need you to read this *up there*," she said, pointing to the podium in front of the casket. I asked her why the minister wasn't doing it. My mom continued, "I found out he can't read English at all. So, *you* have to read."

Before I could answer, she was talking to the minister and pointing over at me. The minister nodded. Following the line of my mom's finger to my face, he came over, asked me how to pronounce my name, and what my relationship to the deceased was. After a quick welcome in Cantonese and English, he called me up.

From behind the podium's sagging microphone, I could see how full the chapel was, mourners shoulder to shoulder across every pew. I wondered how they all knew my grandfather, and why I didn't know any of them. I could see my cousins in the second row, eyes red and faces collapsed. One of them should have been delivering the eulogy. One of them would have written it with stories about a grandfather they had known all their lives, instead of the artless list of facts that I had thrown together. I should have at least reviewed it to be sure I could pronounce the names of his parents and their village, but I was too anxious to unclench the script from my fist. I began by saying that my mom had given me all the facts about my grandfather's life. I sounded like I was blaming her for the boring, stilted sentences I was about to read, like a fifth grader reporting on a forgotten president. I described my grandfather's childhood immigration to California, his marriage, his restaurants, his children, his grandchildren. It all sounded so neat and heroic, a legacy of accomplishments without any mention of what they had cost. Toward the end, I realized I had forgotten to change the wording from what I had prepared for the minister, and that I had been rattling off the shallow details about "Mr. Gee" the whole time like a stranger. Like a granddaughter who had learned nothing from him and had barely been around for the last decade.

Thankfully, the service ended right after I spoke. I hoped everyone thought my voice was shaking from emotion, not from having to read this drivel like the stranger to my grandfather I was. "Nice speech," they whispered as our hands met in the receiving line. "What a history," they marveled politely.

We snaked our cars through the cemetery hills to the grave site. No one spoke as the casket was lowered under the bright California sun. Someone stepped forward to throw in a handful of dirt, then others followed. My cousins all seemed to know how to mourn. They dabbed their eyes and laid their hands for a long time on my grandfather's casket. Their grief was so real. They had all gone to college in the area and gotten jobs close by. All had moved back home with their parents at different times. Since I had stopped going to the restaurant every day, I had seen how other families, even immigrant families, talk to each other over meals, how they're not suspicious or afraid of everything outside their home, how they play with their children and don't blackmail them for affection by threatening to die. Each year, I came home less often, and I recognized the restaurant less and less. I was grateful for the life outside that I had, but I watched my cousins throughout the funeral with disbelief and pangs of envy.

As we headed to our cars again, an usher in dark sunglasses handed out the little red envelopes we had stuffed with money and candy. These were much smaller than the usual ones we filled with money and handed out on happy occasions, only about the size of three postage stamps together and without any good-luck gold characters. A few steps away, another usher stood holding out a battered old tin. My mom told me to take my quarter and eat my candy, then grabbed my envelope and wrapper. "To burn," she said when I reflexively refused to let go and we stood there for a moment, tugging against each other over the debris. I finally let go, and she tossed them both in the tin and received a bow from the usher. Then she pointed at my mouth and said, "Finish your candy now, before you get to the car." She took a long, aggressive drag on the buttery, hard caramel.

I rode in my parents' old minivan toward the repast at the Golden Dragon, a Chinatown institution for dim sum and Cantonese food. Through the heavy westbound traffic, we passed Chinese enclaves like Monterey Park where we didn't know anyone. We would gather that afternoon at someone else's restaurant to eat someone else's food, thankful not to have to think about the labor of its creation. Surrounded by distant family, before a feast swirling across ten lazy Susans, we ate Chinese food we recognized from home—tofu soup, bean curd, steamed fish, grilled abalone, water spinach, and roast duck. There was nothing sweet and sour or resembling chop suey, no crispy fried noodles or fortune cookies. We toasted my grandfather's life and accomplishments with spoonfuls of pale wine after a banquet that none of his customers would have recognized as Chinese.

The restaurant was my first liturgy, and not entirely unlike a Mass. Both are centered around a meal that is received in an orderly line and taken away to be consumed. There are greetings, printed aids, recitations, occasional donations, and blessings bestowed. But the restaurant meal is never shared between the preparer and receiver. Food preparation is a separate and secret liturgy. Components are washed, cut, and stored the night before. The right pieces join together in the flash of a seasoned wok. Efficiency is sacred. Nothing is wasted, not a knife stroke or a salt grain or more than three packets of free soy sauce per order. Not a penny given to round up a payment. Not an ounce more meat when we can pack in cheaper celery, onions, and bean sprouts.

The take-out restaurant's liturgy is harried and hot. We promise it will be good when you get home, that there will be enough to share and for tomorrow's lunch. We evangelize with abundance— rice straining against the carton's tab, everything packed so tightly it erupts when opened. Have all the soda you want. But you have to take it away. You can't stay here, you can't eat in front of us, we won't wash your dishes or pour your water. You cannot bring your wriggling children past the locked door to use our family's bathroom. You cannot use our phone to call your husband who might want egg foo young instead of spareribs this time. The bells that announce you on your side of the counter are the same ones that ring out your departure. When you leave, you still wear your hunger, but now you carry a steaming box of hope, bursting toward your first bite.

⁓

In the eulogy I should have written, my grandfather was born on February 2, 1914, but this is only an American date and we never celebrated it. The online calendars I find say he was born eight days before the full moon in the second month of the year. I wonder if his mother knew the real date on the lunar calendar, if she'd been able to discover whether this would be an auspicious day for her son to be born.

My grandfather was born in a deeply divided China, ruled by vying warlords, only two years after the collapse of the last imperial dynasty. He was born in a province where the Kuomintang army was mobilizing, later to be led by Chiang Kai-shek and called the Nationalist Army. Between them and the communists, a civil war would erupt when my grandfather was thirteen. But he would already be gone by then.

Eight years before my grandfather was born, the Chinese Exclusion Act, already renewed several times by Congress and the Supreme Court since its first passage in 1882, was made permanent in the United States and blocked nearly all Chinese immigration for the next forty years. Eight years before my grandfather was born, a catastrophic earthquake in San Francisco caused massive fires that destroyed many civic buildings and the documents inside, including birth records. Among those who sought to restore their records were citizens, but Chinese residents also rushed to ask for their papers to be "reissued," claiming their records sat in the rubble and ashes too. And not only that, but they also claimed wives and children in China whom they had the right to bring over. Some claimed eight, nine, ten children back home. These men were granted legal status, then sailed back to China and brought those children over, naturalizing them as citizens of what the Chinese had named the Beautiful Country, despite the Chinese Exclusion Act still being in effect.

My grandfather arrived in America sometime around 1926, twelve years old, alone, and carrying a handful of papers that made him the son of a man he had never met. There are stories of paper sons being interrogated for days or weeks at Angel Island, of spending the month-long journey across the Pacific memorizing the right answers to be someone else's son. I had to read these other men's stories in books because my grandfather never told me his. I read about paper sons who were helped into America by an uncle or cousin, but also about paper fathers who preyed on desperate parents, taking their last pieces of gold and their sons to another country. Some of those boys thought they were coming to the United States but were routed to Peru, Jamaica, or Trinidad. Wherever they arrived, after a month or more at sea, the paper sons owed someone boat fare, food costs, transportation to Chinatown, and many other fees their families often had not agreed to. Paper sons labored to dig themselves out of this hole, but it was never enough. In China, agents of paper fathers were known to harass the families who sent away their sons, claiming the boys had reneged on their debts, demanding the parents pay instead.

In Chinatown, my grandfather slept on kitchen floors and the back steps of restaurants. Sometimes he found a bed in a boarding house. Families in Chinatown were stretched too thin for handouts to a nameless boy. There was no one to raise him anymore, just those who participated in his survival or not. Once, my grandfather recalled being ill and unable to leave the apartment of some distant relative who had no desire to care for him. He remembered lying in bed for days, delirious with fever and dehydration. He remembered a broomstick poking him to see if he would stir, then being left to die. All this, and he still thought of himself as lucky to be far away from the horrors of his home country's civil war. He began to learn. Dishes, mopping, inventory, food prep, cooking, serving. Somehow these scraps of story made it to my mom, maybe through my grandmother during long restaurant afternoons. Somehow, they also fell on my table, only to end up tossed with American words.

My grandfather built his restaurant with the highest walls and the fewest windows possible. He did not settle in Chinatown or one of the many inland or valley cities with growing Chinese communities. Instead, he chose an island and built himself a fortress on it. Sent from home only to find himself forever a stranger here, he made his own safety and refuge. I was around him every day for the first thirteen years of my life, and yet I knew nothing at all. All I could do was imagine. Because I didn't know his parents' names, I got a C on my fifth grade family tree project, a red slash through every space I left blank. Besides, who could ever fill the branches above my grandfather? My family begins with him. He was our origin story, our first human formed out of mud and breath. He was pure survival from which we all sprang, severed from any roots, any connection to past, culture, homeland, or ancestors. I can still see him nimbly swirling papery egg roll skins across a blazing wok. I see him devour canned fruits—jellied cranberry, syrupy peaches, and applesauce. I see that he almost enjoys cooking the few times a year he stuffs a chicken with sticky rice and Chinese sausage and roasts it to bronze perfection. All the rest he kept to himself.

⁓

Thanksgiving 2003 was the last time my grandfather came downstairs. I had come home from graduate school for the holiday weekend, and we gathered at the restaurant for an early dinner on Thursday. "Early," my mom decided, "so all the kids can go do what they like." Holiday obligations had grown light, usually kids and parents together for a short while before going off with friends. We hadn't spent a holiday at the restaurant in years. When my grandmother was alive, we always gathered for Christmas, which was also her birthday. My mom and aunt worked just as hard on holidays as when they cooked for customers. On top of their regular work, they made dumplings for days—ground pork tucked inside translucent tapioca flour skins, fried sesame and sweet potato balls, and glutinous rice with mung beans, peanuts, and a salted egg yolk steamed in banana leaves. But this year, the holiday was simple. One cousin brought a turkey he had roasted at home, one brought a pie, and my parents brought crackling pork and roast duck from the Chinese barbecue. My mom lit one wok and cooked a small dish of clear noodles with bean sprouts. We ate off paper plates around the little television, sipping on soda cans from the display fridge.

With a little coaxing, my grandfather joined us. He had eaten his dinner alone upstairs, but when my dad came to collect his tray and asked him one last time to come down, he agreed. He used a wheelchair to get out of his room, then descended to the ground floor in the electric stair chair. None of us spoke much. Everyone was eyeing the score of a Lakers game on TV. After a few minutes, my grandfather asked to be taken outside.

"Don't go," we said. "Stay for a little while."

He didn't want to go back upstairs; he just wanted to sit in the backyard.

Someone had brought a camera, and that day we took what would be our last pictures of him. My mom and aunt hated having their picture taken at work. They protested that they looked awful, that they didn't want to see themselves in stained aprons. But we sat flashing smiles among the empty plates and foil cartons. We took one picture of my grandfather sunning himself in the yard. He is in the center of the frame, a small figure in the camera's wide zoom, wearing pajama bottoms, a down vest over a thermal top, and a black knit cap. He is in his wheelchair looking off to the side, though in my memory we are all standing around behind the camera, clicking our tongues at the overgrown yard, the piles of cardboard yet to be hauled to the recycling center. Each of us probably could have guessed that we had only a few more years here. Behind my grandfather is our lemon tree, the last of the poor garden that never did bear sweet fruit. The sun is bright and he is squinting, his hands at rest, his mouth slightly open. Around him, tarps cover small hills of beer boxes used to pack up orders. Bleached aprons and dishrags crisp in the sun. The yard hums with all manner of creatures allowed to make homes in its neglected wilderness, including a colony of bees in an exposed pipe, a feral cat with her scrawny litter, roaming possums, and dusty orange butterflies draping the chain-link fence and flimsy passion fruit vines. Every one of them had crawled or winged its way here to shelter in a declining restaurant's backyard, surviving on what was provided, what they could fashion, and all they had learned to live without.

PRETTY LITURGIES

We arrived at the hospital ahead of a February snowstorm with hopes that medication would induce my labor. My body was unbothered by the medical advice against carrying a baby past forty-one weeks, and it wasn't until four hours after the second administering of Cervidil that my contractions started. Eighteen hours after checking in, I had progressed enough to receive an epidural. The relief was immediate and blissful, but an hour later, the monitor with the baby's heartbeat fell blank. A nurse fumbled under my blanket and around my legs, asking, "Where's your button, hon?" again and again until she pulled up the emergency call button like a fishing line. Suddenly a dozen hands were lifting me by my bed sheet onto a gurney and wheeling me into an operating room as my husband interlaced his fingers on top of his head, his arms bent into panicked triangle wings.

As I watched a blue drape rise to separate me from the lower half of my body, someone offered me a gloved hand. Not a medical glove, but one that was loose fitting and textured, like you would wear to serve food. It dampened quickly from my grip. I didn't let go until the C-section was over, not even after they finally let Paul in and he cemented his forehead to mine for the rest of the procedure. I hoped, vaguely, for my daughter and me not to die. I also hoped not to feel the incision. After some incredible pressure on my abdomen, a tiny gray body flashed above the drape. There was a long silence before she rasped and coughed, and they whisked her to the NICU for oxygen and fluids. In the meantime, I had lost all sense of my body, all feeling gone except for uncontrollable shivering and teeth chattering from the medications. In the recovery room, I was crazed with thirst but not cleared to ingest anything yet. After refusing me several times, a nurse relented and let me suck on a wrung-out washcloth to stave off the hysteria rising from my slashed gut. I slipped in and out of sleep. When I opened my eyes, Paul was next to me, holding our camera.

"I saw her," he said, smiling. "She's hooked up to tubes, but she looks fine. I took a video."

On the tiny camera screen, she was splayed out under an oxygen tube, with three monitors taped to her chest. Her ID bracelet took up half her forearm. She was also diapered and hatted, flush with color and whimpering a little as Paul rubbed her little arm. A nurse standing above my shoulder said, "Your turn, Mom," as she released the brakes of my bed and wheeled me in it toward the NICU. I felt as big as a cruise ship navigating the hallways and rows of babies in clear tubs. When I saw our daughter, she was a little stranger and half machine, her face obscured by tubes taped to her nose. But we felt good enough to call our families and say she was here, to read them her weight, length, and time of birth that someone had written on a card and taped to the side of her tub. Eight hours after she was born, they took her off all tubes and monitors and brought her to my room, bathed and swaddled and completely perfect.

My husband told me later, as I devoured the Boston Market fried chicken he'd brought, that he ran into the doctor who had operated on me while she was strolling down the hall and eating a sandwich. He stopped her and thanked her profusely, his voice breaking. She suspected a placental abruption—when the placenta detaches too early from the uterus—had cut off the baby's oxygen. Between the mute heartbeat monitor and our daughter's birth, fewer than ten minutes had passed. The doctor told my husband we had been very lucky. She added, "It might have been disastrous." Paul couldn't get the word out of his head, or the image of her heading into the rest of her day with that sandwich. What lives she would encounter next? Which would she save? Which might slip beyond her? I wondered what other hands would cling to an aide's glove, as mine did while the doctor saved our lives, and when they would finally let go. I hoped the doctor's sandwich sustained her.

Then Paul said, "You're going to think this is weird."

"What?"

"I went to the hospital chapel," he admitted, "before I went home last night to shower." He hadn't planned to, but something beckoned him as he passed the open doors on his way to the parking lot. He ended up sitting for a while in the rotunda of waiting room seats. "I just sat there and said 'Thank you,'" Paul explained. "I didn't have any other category to express what I was feeling."

I didn't yet have an organizing principle for gratitude. Mine was still swirling among my nervous overwhelm, exhaustion, and suddenly ravenous appetite. I was still barely able to make out the mysteries of new parenthood in relief and the shadow of *what if*. Or the luck, science, privilege, and care that had saved us both. We were not yet praying people. We wouldn't be until after my next, much calmer C-section, two and a half years later. But it was comforting to hear that my husband had a container the right size and shape for his gratitude in that chapel.

We had no plans to baptize our daughter, and there was no other ritual I knew of, no ceremony or celebration for this new life and the new family we had become. But then I called my mom when my daughter was a week old and asked, "You know that red egg party for babies? Do you want to do that?" In China, a new mother stays in bed and in confinement for a month while the women in the family feed her dishes filled with liver and ginger. Then, they emerge, the baby ready to be named and brought safely out into the world, and the mother strong enough to resume her life. I vaguely remembered seeing pictures of this ceremony for some cousins' new babies over the years. Other than a red egg party, I didn't know how to bring my daughter into the world, ceremonially speaking.

"You know how to do the ceremony?" I asked my mom.

"We can come," she replied.

I thought she might call her sister, Auntie May, who was eighteen years older and a grandmother of several who had received red egg ceremonies. Auntie May was who we called for traditional recipes or instructions on how to set out ancestor offerings correctly on our mantle. She was the one who loaded our car with fuzzy melons that only she could grow to taste like their childhood.

Growing up, we visited Auntie May two or three times a year, my dad driving our station wagon up the spine of California from our Los Angeles suburb to the Mangan Park neighborhood of Sacramento where my mom's entire family lived. There, my mom savored foods I never saw at home—gnarled bitter melons, soy sauce eggs, feathery squash blossoms. At home, my mom usually cobbled together restaurant leftovers with the little time she had to cook for me after cooking all day for customers. Sometimes she made me a steaming bowl of rice topped with a velvety raw egg yolk or soup with noodles and chicken livers. But in Sacramento, she was suddenly able to braise and season exotic leafy greens and neck bones. She soaked dried scallops for rice porridge and trimmed translucent wood ear mushrooms. My mom grew very young when we visited her mother, sister, and brothers. The youngest of five, she returned to that role around her family—serving, deferring, asking permission. They alternately lavished attention on her and ignored her. Her Cantonese softened within a few hours of being among her siblings, dropping the harsher tones and higher volume of my dad's more guttural family dialect. In Sacramento, my mom relaxed into her siblings' rhythms, expectations, and traditions, seeming more herself than anywhere else. She seemed lighter and less worried about me. She seemed to be carrying less.

When my parents arrived at my home in St. Louis for my daughter's party, my mom handed me a printout of a website's directions, "How to Throw a Chinese Red Egg and Ginger Party." The website was in English. It mentioned that eggs were a symbol of new life, that the party also marked the end of a Chinese mother's thirty-day confinement after giving birth, and that the baby and guests should wear red. It was a website I would have used myself if I were trying to throw the party. Clearly, she hadn't talked to Auntie May.

The morning of the party, my mom boiled three dozen white eggs. She filled a coffee mug with water and red dye from a Dollar Store kit she had brought, which looked exactly like the ones I had used in school for Easter eggs. Even the little wire wand for submerging and lifting out the eggs was the same as I remembered. The eggs came out a deep shade of brick red and she piled them into a mixing bowl rummaged out of my pantry.

Paul's family drove in from Illinois, and the twelve of them and my parents squeezed into our brick bungalow, where I had carefully hung a four-foot silk embroidery scene of a hundred white cranes, the same one all my relatives and every Chinese kid from school displayed in their homes too. This, like the red-tasseled door charms, the zodiac animal carvings, and the jade pendants in my jewelry box, was my small invitation to the Chinese part of myself that only occasionally got acknowledged. The culture of my childhood home was more immigrant than anything else, and it felt as loose as paint shedding from sun-scorched California stucco.

My daughter's red egg party lasted approximately two minutes. With the entire family crammed around our dining room table, I brought out the baby, dressed in a red silk jumpsuit my mom had brought that hung beyond her skinny newborn frame, complete with impossible frog buttons and drool stains. The soft matching cap, thickly bordered with gold, looked like a rice bowl over my daughter's inky hair. She wailed the whole time, probably over-tired, overstimulated, half-filled with my disappearing milk and overflowing anxiety. I held her out tentatively at my mom. She took one red egg and drew it across the tiny forehead, around the cheeks blistered with baby acne, over the trembling red mouth. She barely touched the baby's skin—it was more like passing a black light or metal detector over her. As she did, my mom chanted, "leng, leng." After several passes, my mom returned the egg to the bowl. I hoisted my whimpering daughter onto my shoulder, and the room broke into uncertain applause. The ceremony's only words were *pretty, pretty.*

—

We followed a few old village customs throughout my childhood, cleaning the house, venerating ancestors, and leaving the porch light on overnight for the Lunar New Year. I never knew whether the light invited or repelled spirits. I wasn't allowed to bathe on either the Lunar or Gregorian New Year. And I was forbidden from saying or thinking bad thoughts, taking the broom out of the closet, refusing to eat good-luck food, or wearing a sour expression. We lit incense, lined the fireplace mantle with tangerines, and hid away our shoes. Other than these gestures, I knew nothing of Chinese rites or rituals.

I got married without a traditional Chinese tea ceremony. No one asked us to have one, and I had only a vague sense that some of my cousins had prepared and served a perfect cup of tea for their parents and in-laws as a promise of lifelong filial piety. As my husband and I planned our wedding, my mom never made any demands or gave any input. When I asked if her friends and relatives would like a reception of Chinese food, she said, "Whatever you want." I asked if the museum in Pasadena we had chosen for our venue would be convenient enough for guests, and she replied, "Do what you like." Unable to express anything she wants directly, my mom will hint: "It's nice to invite kids too." Or she will warn: "It's outside? May is a very hot month." Maybe she did tell me how I could bring Chinese customs into my wedding, in a way I no longer wanted to hear. I chose a long Chinese cheongsam for my gown, in traditional red silk but with an untraditional curl of colorful flowers embroidered down the skirt front. My mom said my dress was leng, even though it didn't have sleeves or a pattern of good luck symbols. There are no superlatives for leng. The word contains *beautiful*, *lovely*, *gorgeous*, *cute*, *stunning*. Leng, like so many Cantonese words, translates differently depending on context. When describing food, it means *appetizing*. For a car, it denotes *impressive*. Our American caterer would prepare a buffet of lo mein, fried rice, pot stickers, and beef with broccoli, while a cousin planned to pick up twenty pounds of crackling pork belly from a local Chinese barbecue. All these touches skirted the cultural edges of my otherwise completely American wedding with jazz musicians and assorted pies.

When I mentioned in an email that my bridesmaids would wear black dresses and carry red flowers, my mom called me in a panic. "It's so they can wear something they already own," I explained impatiently. "Or buy something they'll wear again." But my mom was adamant that black at a wedding was an egregious bad luck display and would invite lifelong misfortune. Black on women, she clarified. Black men's suits were fine. "I've already told the girls," I said about the bridesmaids. My mom began sobbing so hard I could hardly make out her warning that black dresses enrage ancestors and result in tragedy—husbands leaving their wives or children getting cancer. "Why would you want to *do* something like that to yourself?" she cried.

After I hung up and recounted the conversation to Paul, I prepared myself to die on this hill. I had longed for my mom to guide me through some kind of wedding tradition. I had wanted instructions on how to join or serve something larger than myself, not just a capricious policing of my color palette. But these were ancestors, always vengeful and exacting, impossible to please and offended by our slightest failure, omission, or lack of vigilance. It was only when she was afraid that my mom insisted on tradition, that she asserted what it was to be Chinese.

Paul said gently, "If it doesn't make *that* much of a difference to us, then maybe we can just let her have this."

His compassion softened and annoyed me. Just then, my dad's number flashed across my phone. My dad has never, ever, called me himself. His job is to dial my number, hand the phone to my mom, and chime in loudly over her shoulder when she doesn't know a word in English. When I call my parents, my dad will pick up with, "Hi, hang on," and race the phone to my mom without another word. But he called me that day to tell me my mom was really upset. "It's not nice, what you're doing to your mom," he said. He never asked me to change the dresses, but his call was so startling that I said, "Fine, they won't wear black."

He exhaled. "Okay, thank you very much," he said and hung up.

As with all rituals from my childhood, the color of my bridesmaids' dresses was entirely about what to avoid and not what to invite. I ended up asking them to wear silver. They each looked radiant, but I took undue delight in my cousin's choice, a silver satin with wide straps, a ruched bodice, and a knee-length skirt covered with a delicate layer of semitransparent but unmistakably black mesh. As of this writing, she and I have both been happily married for over sixteen years.

—

When my grandmother died in 2006, my mom walked around her Sacramento neighborhood looking for the oldest Chinese ladies who might remember what Chinese people do when someone dies. My grandmother's funeral was a pastiche of things ancient, borrowed, and invented. The rituals included tying black strips of cloth around our forearms, threads of the ripped material dangling as long as the ties themselves. Someone silently guided us into a line to process out of my uncle's house and to our cars. I realized we were being placed in descending order of age. A nondenominational but Christian-influenced service was held in the funeral home's blank template of a chapel. The Chinese pastor assigned to our service spoke about heaven and my grandmother's soul but never mentioned her name. At the grave site, right before my grandmother's casket was lowered into the ground, a few elders stood and turned their backs to the burial. The rest of us quickly did the same without knowing whether our turning away was a sign of respect, fear, or defiance. There was no program, just leaders and followers, and the divide seemed to be generational, between those who had grown up in China and those in America. When I was a new Catholic, I moved through Mass this way, taking my cues from others, startled out of my thoughts, and always half a step behind. Only after years of attending have I finally managed to memorize most of the Mass. Had I years to attend Chinese funerals, maybe I would have grown into them the same way.

At the repast, also in my uncle's house, a card table held a framed black-and-white photograph of my grandmother, her face a near-perfect match for my mom's face, her hair cropped at her ears, her thin nylon shirt high collared, with a faded floral print. One folding chair was tucked under the table. The thick fireplace mantle was lined with fresh incense and oranges, and ceramic planters filled with plastic flowers. My aunties and their neighbors had prepared dozens of dishes with muted colors and flavors. I filled my plate with glassy noodles and steamed chicken, and took the only seat available, at the card table with the photograph. Swiftly, an older cousin picked up my plate and guided me by the arm away from the table. She moved me gently and silently to perch on the arm of the couch, without acknowledging what I eventually figured out was my faux pas. I looked back, mortified that I had plopped my lunch down at my dead grandmother's makeshift altar, but also noting how misleading it was to set a matching folding chair beside it. I wondered if the empty seat was for my grandmother or another ancestral visitor or some other purpose altogether. I wished for a museum sign to orient and educate me.

I think about the elders who ushered us through my grand-mother's funeral. Perhaps they, like my mom and grandmother, had arrived in the swell of immigration after 1965, which would have made them middle-aged when they started their new lives. Or perhaps they had somehow pressed into California during the 1930s, like my own paternal grandfather when he was a twelve-year-old paper son of a stranger. They would have forced their way into a new life without time or opportunity to hold onto the old one. Those elders had nothing like a church to encode or sustain their liturgy, nothing but their two hands to carry every practice that made them Chinese. How heavy they must have grown with each passing year. How eagerly their children would have laid down their share of the weight. My mom didn't stay in Sacramento long enough after her mother's funeral for those ladies to pass her their heavy knowledge. All of us grandkids were grateful for the burst of guidance, but what were the chances we would remember any of it for our own parents' funerals in the coming years? We watched like spectators, carried through the worship and veneration and grief with wide American wonder.

During every childhood trip to Sacramento, my parents and I made visiting rounds to elders close and distant, which I always dreaded. Every great-auntie and -uncle received a half-hour visit, a tin of cookies, and well wishes from the Southern California family. We managed to knock out all the visits in one exhausting day. In these houses, as in her siblings' houses, my mom relayed and received family updates on jobs and babies and divorces. Many offerings of prosperity and longevity were exchanged. No one ever spoke of China. No one spoke of immigration. No one spoke of ties or chains, of longing, grief, fracture, bitterness, alienation, gratitude, remorse, opportunity, relief, assimilation, or the cost and the dream of it all.

⁓

The philosopher James K. A. Smith defines *liturgy* as a set of formative practices that shape our desires, imaginations, loves, habits, and our definitions of human flourishing and the good life. Using Paul Tillich's term, Smith writes, "Liturgies are rituals of *ultimate concern*: rituals that are formative for identity, that inculcate particular visions of the good life, and do so in a way that means to trump other ritual formations." Liturgy, he continues, "subtly but powerfully shapes and aims our desires." As "liturgical animals," we cannot help but organize ourselves toward what we love, nor can we keep one desire from rising above all others. "To be human is to be the kind of creature who is oriented by this kind of primal, ultimate love—even if we never really reflect on it." Though they might have said it was health, happiness, or prosperity—the three wishes bestowed on everyone—safety was my parents' ultimate concern. All the rituals of my childhood, all the symbols, jewelry, food, phrases, and colors imbued with the power to block harm, were outlets for their persistent low-grade fear. As a middle-class American kid as safe as I could be, my parents' measures were lost on me.

I had wanted a red egg party for my daughter because I had been hungry for liturgy all my life. I had wanted to know where I belonged and to whom, to be shaped by rituals and not left to my own formation. As a new mother, I wanted to know what to do at these big life milestones, to help my daughter form her identity because I had known what it was to long for a guide, to wing most decisions and hope for the best because my family's concern had been survival, not flourishing. What did it matter to my parents how I spent my birthdays, whether we gathered for holidays, or how a baby is welcomed with red eggs when we were all miraculously alive?

I had expected my mom to know how to ritually welcome her first grandchild, that she would have picked it up somewhere between fleeing China in 1959 and languishing in Hong Kong until 1966, between arriving in the United States without a high school diploma, between cannery work, sweatshop work, and moving from Sacramento to Los Angeles to cook for her new father-in-law's take-out restaurant in 1968.

James K. A. Smith warns that liturgy cannot be a private affair, that it must be communal or social. Nevertheless, my mom alone held the standard of what it meant to be Chinese. She was the one who insisted we store gravesite offerings outside to keep the dead from entering our home. She commanded that we eat chicken for luck and long noodles for long lives on every birthday or anniversary. She draped me in gold and jade for protection and forbade me from wearing black clothing or white hair bands. All those customs, dragged across the ocean when my mom was twelve years old, were hers to carry. As with all our silent Chinese observances, I wanted to believe that participating in a red egg ceremony would connect me and my daughter to a place that, however far away, was real and shared. That all our mysterious behaviors meant something somewhere. My dad and I had always obeyed, but we were never participants. I was baffled at why no other Chinese kids I knew were subject to these practices, why they seemed to exist only in our house. Still, my mom practiced good luck and bad luck rituals as if doing them right meant something fragile would hold just a little longer.

My mom is Chinese until she is not. She must do figures in her head in Cantonese; she must eat rice with every meal, fearfully appease ancestors, and call my husband American, but never herself and never me. Until she visits China after forty-five years of living in America and is told that her clothes and hair and speech and posture are all unmistakably foreign. Until she is interviewed by an adoption agency and must, against all her Chinese sensibilities, express her longing for a child. Until she plays matchmaker between her niece in Guangdong and a widowed friend in Orange County, only to be stained with the bad luck of their unhappy match. Until her mother dies and her daughter moves away, and no one remains to exchange or obey or observe. Without anyone to share the burden of culture or the enactment of liturgy, my mom puts her arms out and lays down what she has been carrying on her own all this time. It is shapeless as smoke. A signal, a residue, a by-product of something elemental and devouring.

I am Chinese until I am not. I am asked by strangers where I am really from when "California" is not a good enough answer. People greet me with "ni hao" as if they are doing me a favor. They tell me I look "exactly" like their Japanese or Thai or Vietnamese friends. If it comes up that I spoke Cantonese as a child, they cry, "Ooh, say something," as if my first language is a parlor trick. I am assumed to be from elsewhere, assumed to speak otherwise. And I walk through the world feeling a little bit foreign. Until I am confronted with how very little my broken and childish Cantonese can convey. Until I have nothing to contribute to our city's Lunar New Year celebration. Until Chinese people I meet are openly crestfallen— heartbroken, really—to hear that I do not speak Cantonese with my parents. Until I am asked at Mass to translate and read the prayers of the faithful *in my home language* and I offer to do it in Spanish because I am fluent in Spanish. I kept my Chinese last name when I married so that my name and face would match. I gave each of my daughters a family surname for their middle name. What I carry for them is paper thin, scrawled and crumpled.

~

At Mass, I experienced the opposite of winging it. The liturgy could not be more explicit. With a few exceptions, the priest and the parishioners said the same words in the same order every week, chanting, singing, and reciting at our given times. Even our greetings and goodbyes were scripted. When I first started attending Mass, I struggled with how out-of-place the liturgy could make me feel as I stumbled, lost my place, and said the wrong words at the wrong time. But I also discovered a comfort, safety, and sense of belonging in the Mass. I followed along with the full script, or the Order of the Mass, until I began to remember the parts. I usually gazed at the other parishioners, awed by our togetherness, that we had all woken up that morning and made it here to carry out this liturgy.

An elder at my parish once told me we move through the Mass like a communal meal. We gather and are welcomed, we sing, share stories, give thanks, eat, give thanks again, and go forth sustained. The liturgy did sustain me when Mass felt tired, empty, or patriarchal. Exhausted and ungrateful, I could still sing the Gloria. In a church full of strangers, in the city where I live or one I was passing through, the predictable liturgy and the presence of other worshippers were profoundly settling. As I grew familiar with the rhythms, I found that I could forget about them, and suddenly I could experience something more than the words or the standing and kneeling. The rote movements grounded me with the other bodies while freeing me from all our bodies. I could listen for something beyond the Mass, something that could only be apprehended while I was fulfilling my part.

It was the shared ritual that called me, that kept me coming back even before I fully understood why I had shown up. Joining my parish filled a hunger whose pangs I had mistaken for wanting the wrong things and wanting too much. Before I could articulate why, I was ready to aim my desires alongside my fellow parishioners—toward each other, toward hospitality, inclusion, encounter, and mutual obligation. I could and had certainly tried to do all these things on my own through work or volunteering. But a liturgy that defined human flourishing as equal to what we provide the least among us made the stakes real for me, grounded in our rough human edges, all our failures, forgiveness, and belonging.

⌇

The weekend of the red egg ceremony ended with dinner at the only Cantonese restaurant in our part of the city. It's no accident that we bought a house three blocks away after seeing the gleaming, whole ducks hanging by their necks in the window and the egg tarts in the pastry case. Whenever my family and I go for an early weeknight dinner, the owner's wife pets our girls' heads, presses sweets into their hands, and treats us to orange slices or red bean cakes. The owner's wife is from a part of Guangdong near my mom's village, and they speak the same dialect. The owners have a daughter who moves easily between Cantonese and English, who used to spill her toys and ride her tricycle freely among the diners. I think I am a somewhat alarming vision of what their daughter could become: barely functional in Cantonese, living two thousand miles from my mother, unable to cook traditional Chinese food. But I think they also see hope for her American future of independence and choices. In their girl, I see an uncanny version of my life, one that will continue to be created as long as immigrants continue building lives here.

Our liturgy begins when the glass doors chime, and we enter. We greet the owner's father, chopping crackling pork belly at the roasting station. The TV is on but muted, flashing a classic NBA game with glitchy captions that can't keep up with the announcers. Warm, meaty air ignites our hunger. *The grace of our Lord Jesus Christ, the love of God, and the communion of the Holy Spirit be with you all.* My mom steps to the front of our group to catch the eye of the owner's wife. Having served food all her life, my mom will not hesitate to send back overcooked seafood or waterlogged noodles. She offers the owners gifts of candied tangerine rinds and ginger lozenges. Our tables are chosen, two to fit all sixteen of us. We dance around the chairs and the children, slinging coats and stashing purses. We sit with the ones who need us and the ones we have missed. Who orders? Who pours the water from the already sweating pitcher? Who asks for forks? *Lord, have mercy. Christ, have mercy. Lord, have mercy.*

We recite the names of dishes we love, and hope others love them too, because no one can have their own; no one will taste just a single flavor. We spin water glasses on the lazy Susan into everyone's reach. We spin to distribute plates and napkins. The owner's wife drops a pile of forks in the center of the table and doesn't watch to see who takes one. *Glory to God in the highest.* We say yes to Coke and no to hot tea until my mom orders hot tea and then we all order it too. Then we ask for egg rolls and crab rangoon and pot stickers. We ask for noodles, fried rice, General Tso's chicken, garlicky greens, and egg foo young. The owner's wife smiles at each dish's name as if it were exactly what she would have ordered too. She asks if the kids would like juice boxes, if the adults would like Tsingtao beers. Yes, yes, please. My mom takes her aside and asks for two good luck dishes, soy sauce chicken and whole steamed fish. *Lord, hear our prayer.* My new daughter sleeps in her car seat, and we tuck her under the table where it is dark and quiet, where she will be shielded from crumbs. My in-laws tell my mom the ceremony was beautiful. They tell her they love my daughter's outfit, the hue of the eggs, this restaurant, this family. They tell my mom about their kids; they listen to her tell about how she knows how to cook all of this food. *The word of the Lord. Thanks be to God.*

The owner's wife comes to chat with my mom in rapid Cantonese, which sounds like they are scolding and bickering. At one point my mom says, "Restaurant life is hard." The owner's wife agrees with a low "Mmm." And that is all they say about it. Our dishes arrive, one then two then all ten crowding our tables so we have to stand to serve, pour, and be served, passing and scraping saucy platters of meats and vegetables. We cut small pieces and wipe little mouths and hands. We fill and offer, we pass, we spin and spin. Any concerns over decorum are forgotten in this most American of rituals: going out for Chinese food.

As they always do, people watch to see if my mom likes the food, but she betrays nothing, eating with her chin tucked down as she always does. This is the same food she cooked and loaded into take-out cartons for forty-five years, and it must be the measure of a particular distance she has long navigated. The Chinese food we love is utterly American and unlike anything she grew up eating. This food gave us a life here but kept her in the restaurant sometimes twelve hours a day. This food was her labor and not her vocation. *The Body of Christ. Amen.* Retired now, my mom is served food by a younger mirror of herself, who is living the same labor. And she is anxious about being waited on, about eating this meal, about our loud and messy communion. She does not believe, to this day, that her lifetime of serving others is over. That she can now sit down in front of hot food and be satisfied. How do you come to know this when your daily liturgy has been endless preparation? When you have known how to do *for* but never *with*?

Sated, we argue over the check hiding beneath dozens of fortune cookies. The owner's wife, who already knows we will be in for our usuals on Thursday night, sees my eyebrows arch and pushes the slip toward me. *Go in peace, glorifying the Lord by your life.* I am not yet a praying person, but I am the mother of a daughter now, and I know what it is to hope beyond reason or fear. Until now, a mother's hope has felt like a yoke. It has felt like dragging something ancient and faceless behind me to plow rows for which I have no seeds. My mom's hope was fierce and desperate and single-handed. Her hope was that she alone would have enough to give me because she alone was the remaining source. And now she flutters around the tables as usual, making sure our leftovers are boxed and ready to take, and that there are enough cookies to go around. All around my tiny daughter, our faces glistening with food and joy, her two families have come to welcome her. *Thanks be to God.* We pull my mom's sleeve and say, "Come, sit." We say, "Relax, join us." And then she does.

INVITATIONS

The first church service I ever attended was at my cousin's Chinese Christian congregation, which gathered in the assembly room of our local junior high. "Maybe you'll make some friends," my cousin offered as we pulled into the parking lot, which immediately set my seventh-grade self on a mission not to make friends. At the time, I had only the barest knowledge of the Nativity story, Genesis, and Noah's Ark, all acquired from Christmas songs and claymation classics. The show *Highway to Heaven* shaped my image of angels. A white, leather-bound King James Bible lay flat on our TV stand at home, under a bowl of plastic fruit, because my parents liked the look of the glittery gold fore edge. With so little knowledge or context, I couldn't decipher the satire in the movie *Dogma*, which came out in my junior year of high school. And while my friends convulsed on the floor watching the Monty Python movies, I was at a total loss, thinking only that Christianity looked like a mean and hypocritical mess. I was, in every sense of the word, unchurched.

I went to school with many Korean Presbyterians, Filipino and Vietnamese Catholics, and Chinese evangelicals, but my classmates never evangelized. Outside of their church communities, they never really talked about God at all. They told me church was like language school, a place their parents dragged them to stay in touch with their culture. They attended dutifully but, except for our high school's ecumenical Christian Club, which held prayer lunches and movie nights for those who already believed and belonged, church was something separate from my friends' public-school lives. Their Easter picnics and Christmas potlucks were not for outsiders. I had the sense that church was for reinforcing the bonds of those born into their world.

I had only a handful of interactions with Christians. A cousin on my mom's side used to snap at me repeatedly for taking the Lord's name in vain. Having no idea what that meant, I continued exclaiming, "Oh my god!" or "God, that's dope," throughout her visit, and she chided me continuously, finally telling me that she felt sorry for me because I didn't know the truth. One girl at school told me she knew for certain I wasn't going to heaven and prayed with flourish and ceremony over her packed lunch. A good friend raged about the pastor at her Korean church for telling worshippers they needed to "vote like Christians," then holding up a sample ballot with the bubble filled in next to Bob Dole's name. All the while, I had no idea what Christians believed, but found the few representatives I met to be less than inviting.

Despite all this, I said yes to my cousin's invitation, mostly because it would get me out of a long Sunday afternoon taking phone orders at my grandfather's restaurant where both our moms worked. I didn't mind putting on some nicer clothes and mingling with strangers if it meant not sitting listlessly in front of the phone while longing to hang out with my friends.

The worship space of my cousin's congregation took up only a fraction of the assembly room, demarcated by two sections of folding chairs with an aisle between, a podium, and a projector screen. People said hello to my cousin and smiled at me. When the lights dimmed, we took our seats. A swelling instrumental soundtrack began to play. Across the projector, pictures of majestic mountains and waterfalls flashed, along with images of the Milky Way, a blue human eye, a human embryo, a field of flowers. When the images and music stopped, the lights came up and the pastor appeared at the podium. He was tall, in his thirties, and fluent in English. And he was weeping. He dabbed his eyes with his sleeve and smiled beatifically at us through his tears.

"How can you say there is no God?" he asked us all. He asked it again, several more times, gesturing back to the now-blank screen. His sermon was about God's greatness, about the abundant evidence of God's existence and God's glory. He was moved, in awe. "Do you see it?" he asked, almost pleadingly. "Do you see the works of God? It's so beautiful."

I didn't talk to anyone afterward, and I didn't go back. I was unpersuaded by the pastor's reasoning that a mountain proved the existence of God. Also, I found his imploring suspect. Why was he begging us to agree that God exists? Why was he so desperate to make us feel like any doubt would be a betrayal of our own eyes? The whole service seemed to scold: *If you don't see this, there's something wrong with you.* But, if I'm honest, it was his crying that had repulsed me. I never saw anyone in my family, certainly not men, crying, let alone weeping with abandon and without shame. My mom hated when I cried. It agitated and panicked her, and she did anything she could to make me stop, including candy, promises of candy, or hissing that crying was very bad luck that day—and there was never a day when crying was not bad luck. Once, I cried bitterly on my dad's birthday, because we'd had a disagreement about something and he'd called me a "chiu nui doy," which means something like *brat* in Cantonese and can be translated as "mean," "nasty," or "bad-tempered girl." Forgetting what day it was, I told my mom what he had said when she found me sniveling in my room, thinking she might take my side. But she only demanded I stop crying immediately. "What kind of girl cries and brings bad luck on her father's birthday?" When I couldn't stop, she became enraged. "It's too late! Cry harder then!" The day could not be salvaged. My crying had ruined any chances of receiving prosperity, fortune, and longevity, and had put us all in danger of calamity. And so, I rejected any notion of God or God's works that would induce tears. I wouldn't risk believing in a God who would overwhelm me and wreck my already tenuous chance at happiness.

I didn't attend another church service until the spring of my sophomore year in college, this time a Catholic Mass with a dorm friend who suddenly felt the urge to make it to the 11:00 p.m. Palm Sunday service. Her invitation had been casual. She had said something like, "Shit, I have to go to church tonight. Come with, yeah?" It was no big deal and had nothing to do with what I believed or didn't. It was time together, the hour late enough that we weren't embarrassed to walk with arms linked, young women giving each other courage and permission to pass through the dark city. In those years, freshly away from home, on a sprawling campus that vibrated with possibility, everything felt meaningful. Every friendship, grade, decision, or screwup was another stone mortared to my life's path, which I couldn't stop scrutinizing for clues to its next turn or final destination.

The university's Newman Hall was a low brutalist structure, its concrete surfaces rough and unfinished, except for the floors and the altar, which had been worn to a soft glow. That night, the church was lit only by candles. I fingered the sharp sides of my palm frond, freshly peeled from my friend's. I wouldn't know for more than a decade that we held them at this Mass because disciples had welcomed Jesus into Jerusalem by waving palm branches. At the time, I only worried that my athleisure wear was completely inappropriate for church. I had no idea what anything meant, what I was supposed to do, or if everyone could tell. But I felt warm as my friend's shoulder brushed mine each time we knelt or stood. Though the Mass was in English, I could hear her whispering prayers in Spanish, as she had done throughout her childhood in the small farming town of Salinas.

We sat on the church's balcony, and when the priest came by to shower us with holy water, the spray couldn't reach our seats. He shot us an apologetic glance, made a dry flicking gesture up toward our seats, and winked as if to say we were covered anyway. The service ended near midnight. Students poured out onto Dwight Way, heading for dorms or bars. Despite feeling slightly foreign at that Mass, I had been at ease with my friend and left feeling a little closer to her.

A few semesters later, I enrolled in a course called The Bible as Literature. I had not gone to any other Masses with my friend, or any other church service since that Palm Sunday. I wouldn't have drawn a straight line from Mass to a class on the Bible, but browsing the fall catalog, I was drawn to the idea of studying the Bible like a piece of literature. The professor was, unlike many who taught in a lecture hall, a dynamic and engaging presenter. We would read the first five books of the Bible like a novel, applying everything we knew as English majors to the Scriptures—character analysis, themes, metaphors, foreshadowing, symbolism, narrative structure. We would take note of contradictions, plot twists, and dialogue. "The first story in the Bible," my professor said on the first day, "is about separation. The world wasn't created out of *nothing*," he emphasized. "It was *separated* into being." Out of chaos and formlessness, God established order, distinguishing night from day, earth from sky, land from sea. God's first act was to order the abyss into a world that contained opposites. For the rest of the semester, my professor maintained his relentless enthusiasm, mesmerizing us with the story of God and the Bible's storytelling.

It was my first actual glimpse at Scripture, and I was taken by the language and lyricism. I realized that whatever mystery lay behind church doors started with this story. The people going in and out of the many churches around campus, the ones with folded hands taking up our dorm common area with their prayer groups, the ones locking arms to protest the death penalty outside San Quentin prison across the bay—they were all connected to and through *this* story and the people in it. It was a story that provided reason and purpose behind religious practices of reenacting a meal, lighting candles, reciting prayers, and consuming bread and wine, all a stark contrast to the rituals of my childhood. Whatever my family did to appease or tempt or revere our ancestors lived apart from any story that my mom could remember or tell. We didn't even know the names of our ancestors. My mom gave no reason for why certain foods were mandatory for good luck, why failing to make them would be not just an absence of good luck but an invitation for ancestors to curse us, why leaving our shoes out during the new year was a guarantee of a year's misfortune. Absent the narrative grounding of any origin stories, I performed these inchoate and ominous rituals quickly and half-heartedly, equating them with not walking under a ladder or throwing salt over your shoulder. Once I left home, I never gave a thought to lighting incense on the mantle or learning to cook dishes for prosperity. Each Lunar New Year came and went entirely unobserved, with no invitations for either failure or fortune.

—

The Sunday in October 2013 when my youngest daughter turned four days old, my visiting mother-in-law and I sat up together into the early hours listening to the baby's rumbling sleep. As the sun was coming up, she asked, "So, what do you think about Mass today?"

My mother-in-law had been cooking and entertaining our toddler while I tried to nurse, tended my C-section stitches, threw away my breast pump, switched very happily to formula, and settled slowly into the clearing haze of our new life. She had asked casually, with nothing urgent or hinting in her tone. We usually went to Mass with her during our visits to Chicago, to the parish where my husband grew up going to guitar Mass in the school's basement. We had never taken her to church in our city because we didn't yet have one.

But we had spent the last year talking about a book by Gregory Boyle, a Jesuit priest who had founded the gang rehabilitation and reentry program Homeboy Industries in Los Angeles. Paul and I had listened to Krista Tippett interview Boyle on a late-night drive home from Chicago, while our oldest slept in the backseat and the one to come tucked and rolled inside my belly, as deep stretches of corn and soybeans flicked by. Boyle described how his duty as a Christian was to expand the margins out so far that no one stood outside them anymore, as the mutuality and kinship that returned former gang members to themselves also returned Boyle to himself. We listened to the entire podcast twice, wondering how we could both find jobs in LA, become Homeboy volunteers, and grow avocados in our backyard. Boyle's voice filled and warmed me, like a rich meal. He said our calling was to stand in awe of what people must carry instead of standing in judgment at the way they carry it. He said that we each had, as Dorothy Day said using John Ruskin's words, a "duty to delight." There was more about attachment repair and compassion and where we find the sacred. For weeks I couldn't stop thinking about this interview. It was like a new phrase of music I could not unhear, there in the car carrying our whole life down I-55 toward home. Paul and I read Boyle's book, *Tattoos on the Heart*, over and over again, not thinking of it as Christian belief so much as just a way of living that made sudden sense, that we wanted to be part of.

That spring, as my belly expanded with our second daughter, Pope Francis was elected to head the Catholic Church—the first Jesuit and first South American to hold the papacy. The change mattered to Paul, though he had been alienated from the church for over a decade. The sexual abuse scandal in Boston had been his last straw, and it was with as much heartbreak as anger that he walked away from the faith in which he was raised. By the time we met in 2004, Paul and I both described ourselves as atheists. And yet, that Christmas, his gift to me was a copy of C. S. Lewis's *The Screwtape Letters*, a series of biting, satirical letters from a senior demon named Screwtape to his hapless nephew, Wormwood, a tempter-in-training whom Screwtape mentors as he tries to prevent his human "patient" from becoming a Christian. "This might seem weird," Paul said as I tore off the wrapping. "But it's an old favorite of mine I wanted to share with you." In our early days in Albuquerque, where we had met as graduate students flung far from our homes in Los Angeles and Chicago, we tested love's waters with offerings of our beloved things—books, movies, plaintive nineties ballads, food. Falling in love meant trusting each other with what we loved and who we had become because of them. I loved that Paul had spent his first two years out of college with Jesuit Volunteers International, teaching middle school in Kingston, Jamaica, and that he had gone on retreat in Santa Fe to discern his own possible religious vocation with the Jesuits. He had discovered on that retreat that his vocation was not in religious community but in family life. He had gone through periods of deep religiosity and then a decade of angry alienation, but he had never not been God-haunted. These parts of his formation didn't scare me or give me pause, for however irreligious I may have been, I recognized that our questions and our seeking were moving us in the same direction.

We read *The Screwtape Letters* together, laughing out loud, huffing ruefully, and falling still before our own messy insides rendered uncannily on the page. When I wanted to source Lewis's many Scripture references, I opened the Oxford Annotated Bible I had kept from my college course, overrun with enthusiastic marginalia. I recognized Lewis's Patient, who undergoes religious conversion and falls in love, all the while subject to the hauntingly familiar temptations of envy, rivalry, snobbery, cynicism, contempt, and false piety. As I too was falling in love, feeling called toward something beyond myself, the book was a mirror and invitation to explore who I wanted and didn't want to be. "Maybe, deep down, I had needed to know that we could talk about God," Paul later confessed. "Maybe I needed to know that it still mattered to me and would matter to you, too." We were not people of faith when we started our lives together. And yet, *The Screwtape Letters*. And yet, Paul took a job at a Jesuit university because their mission mattered to him. And yet, I had offered to look into whether and how we could be married by the Jesuit priest who had been his mentor and oldest friend.

After the Gregory Boyle podcast, our seeking turned more concrete. We had always begun with books—for me, Anne Lamott, Mary Karr, Karen Armstrong, and later, Joan Chittister and Elizabeth A. Johnson—but now faith meant edging toward something like a practice, a community, a life. We talked all through my second pregnancy about what that might look like. Would we attend Paul's university church or a neighborhood parish? According to the official archdiocese boundaries, we lived in the territory of a parish two miles away. But there was another one right in our neighborhood, six blocks away. I brought up the Episcopal church we could also walk to, with a married mother of two as the pastor and an active social justice ministry. "I can't," Paul replied. "I'm sorry. It would be like . . . changing my nationality." He then recalled that one day, not long after he had started his new faculty position, he was introduced to a retired Jesuit living in the community's housing. When Paul mentioned going to a Jesuit high school, the priest muttered, "Well, there you go. A dog always returns to his own vomit." Paul was and had always been Catholic, so this is where we would seek our faith community, me for the first time and him for the first in a long time. But we allowed for the possibility that the Catholic Church might not feel like a good home for us. There was so much we remained unsure of, but one thing we agreed on was that, if we made this leap, we would be all in, as we were when we had first moved to St. Louis. We had thrown ourselves into living here, both of us sick of moving nearly every year since college. We decided this would not be a starter city for us. I wanted to be settled, to be somewhere long enough to be *from* that place. So we arrived with the plan that I would find full-time work, we would save for a house, stay during the summers, and get to know the city. If we wanted to belong, then we needed to be here.

But we still had so many questions. Would I get baptized? Would we baptize our daughters? Would we send them to Catholic schools? Had Paul fully processed his anger and alienation? Why, exactly, were we even doing this? We each wondered and wrestled at different times, by turns hesitant and assured, mostly fortified by each other. The only answer we had was that we had been given a way to seek and encounter the transcendent. We realized how radical the Christian faith could and ought to be in its welcome, hospitality, love, obligation, inclusion, and common good. That it could be the opposite of exclusionary and condemning. All summer and fall my due date neared, and we inched toward getting to Mass on a Sunday, just to try it out, just to see. At first, our trepidation kept winning out. I loved our life and good fortune and was nervous about changing it. But the call was there, unmistakable, getting louder: *more*. Not more stuff or accomplishments, but a bigger container for ourselves and our lives. I think we knew that once we went, there would be no going back.

That Sunday after my youngest was born, we were all so sleepless and disoriented inside this new configuration of life. I knew enough about Mass to know that I would remain awkwardly seated while everyone else received Communion. But something said *yes*, and not even to score points with my mother-in-law. Something said *go*. A few hours later, we piled around two bulky car seats, my C-section incision still inflamed around its stitches and my prescription of Percocet tucked in the diaper bag. It was after ten o'clock. Mass at the parish near our house had already begun. We sighed and headed to the university church because they began at ten thirty.

Maybe it was the choir's harmonies lifting into the dark ceiling arches, or my hormone-soaked body, or the fresh newborn and chirpy toddler taking up all our arms that made my eyes well up as soon as we slid into our pew. Or maybe that my body knew it was finished growing babies, that we were, after all these years spent building, suddenly looking at our completed project. A house, a car, two jobs, and two daughters—there was nothing left to chase. The spiritual writer Ronald Rolheiser describes our first spiritual drive as "a struggle for self-identity and private fulfillment." During our youth, we need to search, acquire, and build a new home. After that, he writes, our calling is to figure out how to give our lives away.

I didn't know what I was ready for, only that I felt like the disciple Simon, a fisherman described in the Gospel of Luke, who answers Jesus's invitation to follow him by setting his nets down without hesitation. But not before Jesus, a stranger, tells him to cast out his nets once more, despite knowing Simon had just spent a long night pulling up nothing. Simon obeys, then finds his nets so full they threaten to capsize the boat. I, too, was reaching for something to hold the largeness of my catch. I, too, felt as undeserving as Simon when he turned to Jesus in astonishment and pleaded, "Depart from me, Lord, for I am a sinful man." The poet Christian Wiman describes the new way of seeing faith brings: "My old ideas simply were not adequate for the extremes of joy and grief that I experienced, but when I looked at my life . . . through the lens of Christ . . . it made sense. The world made sense."

Raw and open, I lurched through the motions of that first Mass, standing, responding, and kneeling a few beats behind everyone else. Normally, I would have felt anxious and self-conscious about my out-of-placeness. But that morning, despite the unfamiliarity that surrounded me—the strangers, the ritual, my own altered body and family—I recognized a calm, steady weight around and in me. I felt planted. Even my crying, which, public or not, has always flooded me with embarrassment, here somehow felt like the correct, if mysterious, response to what was happening around and in me. When we came home, Paul and I agreed we would try our neighborhood parish the next week.

It's hard not to wonder if there was a single moment that set me on my way to becoming a person of faith. This calling surprised me with its suddenness and vigor, and then with how quickly it became an anchor in our lives. But it also felt natural, easy, not so much a decision but more of a settling into something already, almost, familiar. Christian Wiman writes of his own religious turn: "I never experienced a conversion so much as an assent to a faith that had long been latent within me." My conversion, which was always a process and never a point in time, felt new and familiar, an aspiring toward a more expansive self, but one I ultimately recognized.

When I look to my childhood for clues, there seems no clear path toward a religious turn, but perhaps my parents' connection to the mysterious had set the dial for my religious attunement. My parents didn't believe in God, but they did believe in ghosts. We lived with the spirits of ancestors, tracing a direct line from our behaviors to their displeasure to our consequences. My mom appeased, served, and honored the dead we remembered and the dead we could only imagine, ever vigilant of their ceaseless inspection and impossible expectations. We never dared ask our ancestors for anything, but when my mom was desperate for her mother to recover from a heart attack, she folded her hands, closed her eyes, and whispered, "Please, please." It was as much a prayer as anything I had ever seen. We didn't have a language for faith, but we did know that we were subject to things more powerful than us, that the world was made up of more than what we could see.

Had they stopped to give it any thought at all, my Chinese parents would have seen church as anathema to many of their values—tithing away hard-earned money, confessing our private business, trusting strangers, contemplating death (and worse, talking openly about it), spending unpaid time on unproductive things like prayer. Having endured famine, immigration, exclusion, and the grief of cultural assimilation, my parents came by their values honestly, and so forbade me to speak of death or bad luck, save anything less than half of what I earned, or venture out among the strangers who might cheat, lie, or take me for a fool. I realize now just how perfect a teenage rebellion religious conversion could have been for me.

I would not say faith was my response to primal absences of liturgy or language, nor that it filled a void or made me whole. It was not a fix but a way forward. "Seekers are those who both lack something for which they are looking, and at the same time possess it in some measure, enough to know vaguely what they are asking for." Roger Haight's definition helps me see a through line where I once imagined there could only be a break with the past. I was, indeed, looking for something, at a time when it seemed I had found everything I could ever want in life. Only, that which I hungered for I had already come with, at least in part. I found something familiar in faith and the Catholic Church, an uncanniness, a mirror. Spirituality, as Haight defines it, belongs to us all, religious or not. It is "a logic, or character, or consistent quality of a person's . . . pattern of living insofar as it is measured before some ultimate reality." Perhaps I finally recognized my spirituality once I could see it in others, in the same way I recognize myself in the features and gestures of my daughters. What the church also gave me was story, ritual, and a way to live according to that ultimate concern which called me both out from and toward myself. To not respond somehow to this call, however muffled, however mystifying, would have felt like turning away from the doors of my home flung wide open. Christian Wiman wonders if "perhaps it is never disbelief, which at least is active and conscious, that destroys a person, but unacknowledged belief."

⁓

About a year after we'd joined our parish in St. Louis, our pastoral associate approached me after Sunday Mass. She was a member of the religious order Sister of Charity of the Incarnate Word, who oversaw ministries and programs at our church.

"Thank you for your email," Sr. M said.

The week before, she'd put a call in the bulletin for open feedback on whatever was on our minds—something we wanted to change, something we wanted more or less of, anything. I knew Sr. M from Mass and all the events she coordinated, from a three-month Bible study to the weekly five-hundred-plate fish fry dinners every Friday during Lent. I responded to her message and mentioned that on my family's registration forms, we had explained the beginnings of my conversion and my husband's return to church. "I thought we'd maybe get a phone call or something," I wrote. At Mass, people smiled warmly at us, but we were mostly left alone. In early January, maybe three months after we'd started attending, another sister, in charge of the potluck lunch after the Feast of the Epiphany Mass, asked me to bring some soup to share. I was glad to be asked, sure that bringing a potluck dish was a sign that we belonged. Other than that invitation to contribute, we hadn't really gotten to know many people in the parish. Most Sundays Paul and I wrangled our young daughters while trying to absorb some of the liturgy, spending long stretches pacing the vestibule or letting the girls tumble around the baptistry room near the back, dubbed the "cry room." We usually rushed home for lunch and naps instead of staying for coffee and doughnuts in the basement. A year in, we finally knew several other families and were feeling more settled in the parish community. But it had been awkward at first.

I felt bad for complaining about all this to Sr. M in my email, but she assured me in person that this was exactly what she wanted to know. "Come to lunch, and you can tell me more," she said.

Paul took the girls home, and Sr. M and I headed down the street to St. Louis Bread Company. We paid for our own sandwiches and slid into a booth by a window overlooking South Grand Boulevard, its quirky shops and restaurants tucked among daily living needs like the post office, library, international market, and our church.

I told Sr. M that I really didn't have any more feedback to add, so we just talked instead. I was intrigued to learn she had become a sister later in life, only ten years before we'd met. She told me she had lived a "regular" life and found it wanting. Owning a home, having a career and money to spend—none of it had felt like it mattered. I told her about my daughters, who were four and almost one, my teaching job at the community college, and having been raised in an unreligious household.

"You joined us last year?" she asked.

"Maybe nine months ago," I replied.

She put her fork down on her compostable plate and asked, "Are you planning to receive the sacraments and enter the church?"

No one had ever asked me this before. People in the parish assumed I was Catholic because I showed up regularly, and they were surprised to learn that I was not baptized. They found it strange that I wasn't on my way to receiving my sacraments and sometimes suggested, "Just do RCIA." When I didn't know what that meant, they explained, "That's, like, the class you take to get baptized." I wondered if anyone noticed that I never went up to receive Communion, nor did I always genuflect before entering a pew, or kneel, or say the right responses. My husband did all these things as easily and naturally as he must have during his twelve years of Catholic school. Meanwhile, I savored the few moments alone while he carried the girls up the aisle, received Communion, and held them each out to receive a blessing. I could never be completely attentive to the liturgy of the Mass, so I snatched wafts of music, incense, and ringing bells when I could, usually while snack puffs disintegrated on the girls' tongues. As much as the liturgy nourished me, pushing me past the dread of dressing and packing up two tiny kids, I was still something of a guest each week.

Sr. M's question made me think of a parishioner I'd watched that spring preparing for baptism, who rose every Sunday before Communion and approached the altar alone to receive a blessing from the pastor, while parishioners extended our hands toward her in blessing too. Then, accompanied by her sponsor, an older member of the parish, she departed to the chapel for the rest of Mass. Another person preparing for baptism presented himself before Mass one Sunday, without any announcement from the priest about what was happening. Instead of the usual entrance procession, the lights dimmed, and the music paused as the parishioner knocked three times from the vestibule, behind the closed wooden doors that hid him from our view in the pews. Two ushers flung the doors wide open, and he walked, solemnly and alone, up to the altar where the pastor asked him what he was seeking. He answered, "Baptism." My cradle-Catholic husband didn't know what this ceremony was. Looking around, it seemed like most people were a little confused and curious about what was happening. This man, too, would be blessed and dismissed each Sunday.

Other than witnessing these weekly dismissals, I knew nothing about becoming Catholic. Only that I felt no urgency to do so. But maybe the better part of a year was a long time to come to church and still not be an official member. Maybe I should have been thinking about what belonging here meant to me. In any case, Sr. M was the first person to ask me if I wanted to, and not presume that I would or should get baptized.

"Maybe," I faltered in my response. "I guess I don't really know what getting baptized involves."

"RCIA is the Rite of Christian Initiation for Adults. It is usually a months-long process," Sr. M explained, "beginning in the fall and ending with the sacraments of baptism, the Eucharist, and confirmation at the Easter Vigil. Let's see, is it September 18th today? That means you'd already be behind in getting started for this season."

I had no idea I could be late for my own conversion.

"Would I get dismissed during Mass?" I asked, thinking of all our hands raised and eyes trained on the two converts I'd seen.

"That's a part of RCIA, yes. You spend that time talking with a catechist about the ways you see God working in your life. You study the Gospels, learn about church history, the liturgical seasons, things like that."

"I would hate to miss half of Mass," I said.

It was the truth but half so. I did especially love the song that came right after Communion when everyone resettled in their seats and found some quiet, open space both deep inside themselves and wholly together. I didn't want to leave Paul with two squirmy kids. But I also shrank at the idea of taking that solo walk every week.

"Well, the part you'll miss is the Liturgy of the Eucharist," Sr. M replied. "Which you can't participate in anyway until you're baptized."

"What do you mean?" I asked. *I'm sitting right there*, I added in my head.

"There's something happening," Sr. M began, and then paused before proceeding more slowly. "It's happening to the ones who have received baptism. But it's not happening to you."

Before coming to this lunch with Sr. M, I had been content, perhaps marginally curious about the sacraments, but satisfied with the state of my faith life. But now my chest filled with hot liquid at the thought of having been oblivious that something was happening to all the baptized and not me during Mass, something no one could see or hear, but that was definitely for them and not for me.

(Later that day, I looked up Sr. M's statement. According to the Catholic Order of the Mass, there are four components to the liturgy: Introductory Rites, the Liturgy of the Word, the Liturgy of the Eucharist, and Concluding Rites. It is during the Liturgy of the Eucharist that the bread becomes Jesus's body, the wine becomes his blood, and worshippers consume both as Jesus instructed in the Gospels. This portion of the Mass begins with the Eucharistic Prayer. According to church teaching, "this prayer is the prayer of the baptized and ordained." *They* are the ones who are called, to whom "something is happening." When I showed this to Paul, who at first didn't believe Sr. M could be correct, he rolled his eyes hard and said, "Even if it is true, that's a terrible way to say it to someone.")

It seemed that no matter how consistently I came or how much soup I made, God was inviting everyone but me. No matter that my family had been asked to present the gifts several times, my unbaptized hands steadying the small crystal carafe of wine and the gold dish of Communion wafers in my two-year-old's delighted grip as we walked them up the aisle and handed them to the priest so he could perform the Liturgy of the Eucharist that wasn't for me. She may as well have said I shouldn't bother coming to Mass since I was missing the important part anyway.

The part of Mass I found most powerful, that I always made sure to recite, even over the girls' fussing, was after the priest proclaimed, "Behold the Lamb of God. Behold Him who takes away the sins of the world. Blessed are those called to the supper of the Lamb." The response from all the kneeling parishioners is, "Lord, I am not worthy that you should enter under my roof, but only say the word and my soul shall be healed." The words come from a Gospel story that appears in both Matthew and Luke, in which a Roman centurion begs Jesus to heal his servant, in one version paralyzed and in the other dying from illness. Jesus offers to come to the centurion's home and heal his servant, but then the centurion, a ranking member of the Jewish people's oppressors, stops Jesus. He tells Jesus that he is not worthy to have him enter his home and asks that Jesus just say the word and the servant will be healed. The centurion humbles himself and submits to Jesus's power and authority, and he does so in front of Jesus's followers. His faith, in a prophet who rebukes and threatens Roman authority, is rewarded. Was my experience of entering this moment of humility *not actually happening*?

Either way, I slipped inside a familiar disquiet that came from navigating, unaccompanied, a world that my immigrant parents found confusing and overwhelming, something I had always done with a mixture of stubborn determination, forced confidence, and plenty of anxiety. I had always figured out for myself how to get what I wanted—a spot on the volleyball team, an after-school job, a spot on the yearbook staff so I could quit the stupid volleyball team, an acceptance to college and then grad school, a teaching career. But I often made embarrassing mistakes because I was unversed in things like tipping at a hair salon. I'd had to slink out to the car where my mom was waiting, promising the scowling stylist that I would return with her tip. I came back sheepishly with only a few crumpled bills because that's all my mom would give me, irritated at the very idea of tipping and that I, for the first time at age twelve, no longer wanted her blunt home haircuts. Once at Walgreens, I tried to help my mom redeem a coupon for a free water flosser, but the cashier pointed out that the coupon said "Free with purchase of $150 or more." My mom argued for several minutes despite both the cashier and me trying to explain. She was convinced the cashier was the only thing standing between her and a free product, and that her daughter was refusing to help her. I came to hate not knowing what I didn't know, being taken by surprise, and realizing that I'd had it completely wrong. I hated the words *I should have known*.

"What about the Easter Vigil?" I changed the subject with Sr. M, maybe as a deflection, maybe searching for a reason to decline RCIA without it being my decision. The Easter Vigil is when most adult converts receive their first sacraments. In our parish, it begins at eight o'clock and lasts around three hours. "My kids are three and not yet one," I continued. "I would like them to be at my baptism, but they would never make it that late at night. Does it have to happen then?"

Admittedly, there's part of me that is obstinate and defiant just for the sake of pushing back. I see it in my youngest daughter too. ("Do you want your nuggets on the pink plate or the blue plate?" "I want steak and I want to get a green plate!") And, as much as I was raised to be and still mostly am a rule follower, I am also driven to do things exactly my way, even when it's neither better nor easier than any other way. I had always defied my mom very quietly, doing what she expected, but never how she expected it. I went to a good college, but six hours away from home. I went to graduate school, but out of state, on loans, and to study poetry. I married a hard-working, devoted man, but he wasn't Chinese. In asking about the Easter requirement, however, I stumbled onto something real. As I thought about it, I *did* want my girls present when I got baptized. Their witness mattered to me as much as anyone's.

Sr. M carefully wiped a fleck of guacamole from the corner of her mouth. She spoke slowly and deliberately. "This is the procedure for becoming a Catholic. You'll know you're ready when all the things that bother you now no longer bother you."

"Sure," I said. "Okay. Right."

I was bothered by her saying *bother*. It felt unserious, like I was swatting at gnats and not asking about sacraments. *I* hadn't even brought up the subject of sacraments. *I* was already acting like a person of faith, so why should I have to jump through hoops now? *I* was not going to beg to receive something others had only because their parents had made the choice for them before their skulls had even fused.

Sr. M and I looked at each other for a quiet moment. "Let me ask you," she said seriously. "When you see others going up to receive Communion, do you have the desire to do the same? Do you have a hunger for the Eucharist?"

I hardly knew how to identify any of my hungers—for community, belonging, purpose, encounter with the divine—let alone speak them to another person. Coming from a home where desires felt dangerous and imposing, the antithesis of sacrifice, I reflexively suppressed or denied them. In the culture of my Chinese family, you said *no* to anything that was offered while expecting the offer to come again and more insistently, for your refusal to be taken as a mere show of politeness. *No* meant *yes*, and *yes* didn't exist. Finally, you received the offer—a cup of tea, a second helping, a red envelope full of cash, a hand-me-down bag—without knowing if you had ever wanted it at all. It wasn't until I met my husband that I came to embrace, even enjoy, telling him what I wanted, and seeing that it made him happy to provide what I asked for. But it wasn't a straight line from there to being able to say to Sr. M that I hungered to belong just as I was. And, until that moment, I would not have named the Eucharist as one of my pressing hungers. I didn't know what, if anything, was holding me back, if I was truly content or just afraid to move forward, to ask for more. I did know that our conversation was making me feel like I had been standing outside the doors all this time when I thought I had been inside.

"I don't know," I replied. "Not at the moment."

"Then, you don't have to rush anything," Sr. M said, her voice softer. "There's one gentleman whose wife and kids are all baptized, but he's not. He comes faithfully and is a well-loved member of our parish, and well loved by God."

I had seen the man, who was of South Asian descent, at Mass often. His very handsome family always sat near the front, and they were always surrounded by friends before and after. But I couldn't hear Sr. M saying to me, "You're fine. You're good. Just keep coming." All I could hear was *despite*. I could attend despite not being baptized. God would love me despite being an incomplete Catholic. But the other thing I heard was, *wait*. For what, exactly, I wasn't sure. Maybe for my girls to grow older, for public attention to horrify me less, for the sacraments to feel less like an obstacle and more like an offering, for myself to be ready with a *yes* that meant only *yes*.

In a lifetime of invitations, sometimes my *yes* has been pure curiosity, other times eagerness to please, fear of rejection, relenting to pressure, accepting a challenge. Sometimes my *no* has been all those things too, or my gut saving me, or my boundaries holding. The exact shape of my faith invitation was not yet clear, but I knew that my *yes* could live inside a pause, a watchful kind of entering. Until my lunch with Sr. M, various messengers had said, *come*. They'd beckoned, *see*. Maybe I had become attuned to those invitations and so could only see the catechism and program requirements Sr. M had presented as a stumbling block or gatekeeper. But what if hers was another kind of invitation, however strained it might have felt at the time? One that said, *You came and you saw. Now what?*

LUCK LET GO

My parents are trying their best not to die. Every day, they swallow supplements and medications, walk for miles, and sip various brewed leaves, barks, and fruit skins. They stay out of the sun, don't drink at all, and usually refuse dessert. The idea of grazing during a holiday party or loosening your belt after a meal is unthinkable, irresponsible. They have earned the very good health they enjoy, and they do this all for me. But I'm not the one who wants them to live forever.

My parents have also added my name to all their accounts for seamless transfers after their deaths and because they didn't work all their lives to lose a penny of their savings to taxes, interest, escrow, or fees. They've given me the keys to their house, their safe deposit box, their bedroom, their bedroom closet, and the safe inside the closet. They give me these keys and accounts to prepare me to live without them, and because neither is prepared to live without the other.

I am amazed at how meticulously they can both prepare for and avoid their deaths. Growing up, they forbade me from saying a friend was "going to kill me" or that I was "starving to death." My dad's parents bemoaned the number four in their restaurant's phone number, the unluckiest of numbers because it was tonally similar to the Chinese word for death. But they consoled themselves because the dreaded four came right before the lucky number eight. When visiting relatives' graves, for just a few respectful minutes, my mom used the plastic bouquet wrapping like gloves so that she never touched the dead's offerings. And whenever the cemetery trash cans were full, she littered the plastic, rubber bands, and packets of flower food next to the graves rather than take the dead's things into our car. Almost anything felt like it could be an invitation or temptation for death to visit us, including talking about the dead. We dutifully burned incense and paper money to them but stopped talking about them as soon as they were gone. To this day, we don't talk about my grandparents, Uncle John, Uncle Allen, cousin Janet, or Auntie Elsa. We honored them with rituals, but the dead were not welcome to dwell in us. Death was a final, permanent, and dreaded separation that three of my grandparents avoided as long as they could, languishing in nursing homes at the end of their lives because they would not decline life-saving measures.

The dead crossed over to a place we feared could come for us next if we spoke out of turn or touched the wrong objects. What I know about those who died when I was young is whatever I learned before they were gone. What I thought I understood about death came from television and movies, a jumble of violence, tragedy, crime investigation, funeral mishaps, and revenge. My education in grief came from soap operas, *ER*, *Steel Magnolias*, *Party of Five*, *NYPD Blue*, and an endless supply of Lifetime movies, my whole frame of reference confined to the maudlin and melodrama. Only outside my family did I ever see weeping, addiction, breaking down in the grocery store, lashing out at school, or therapy. Outside was where people had some kind of response to death.

The Thanksgiving after my youngest daughter was born, my mom brought me a bag of jewelry, as she's done on every visit. This was her way of portioning out my inheritance, more preparing for death without ever mentioning it. That holiday, my girls were two and a half years and just shy of two months old, and my mother-in-law had also driven down from Chicago. The fresh and hazy chaos of bottles and two sets of diaper changes still had a little shine to it. Our home felt as full as it would ever be. My mom and I were putting the jewelry away in my rosewood jewelry box where I kept all her other pieces strewn in careless piles. She added the new pendants she had brought for my daughters, glass octagons etched with each girl's zodiac animal and strung with delicate red thread, a few gold chains from China, and cultivated pearl earrings. She suddenly stuck out her wrist, from which dangled a white gold and diamond bracelet.

"Look." My mom smiled. "You like it?"

"It's nice," I said. The crust of diamonds was elegant and hard to miss.

"I bought this," my mom continued, "with money from selling some gold." She fingered the gems proudly. "Do you want to keep it? For the girls?" She started to undo the clasp.

"Wait, what? You sold what?"

"The price of gold is high now, but it was even higher in the summer. So I sold it then." She beamed with her market savvy.

"Oh," I replied. "Wow."

My mom used to let me sift through her jewelry box, usually after she had come home from the restaurant. While she showered, I'd creep into her closet and lift the gray lockbox from the hidden shelf behind all her hanging clothes. I fished the key from the pocket of her never-worn purple wool trench coat and creaked open the heavy lid. Some jewelry was carefully swaddled in pouches embroidered with dragonflies and fish. Many pieces were organized in the compartments of a weathered plastic pencil box. Removing the top shelf of stud earrings revealed heavier pieces below—gold and pearl pendants, jade bracelets, and yard upon yard of gold chains. Spreading them across her dresser, I would memorize their weights and contours. As she dressed for bed, my mom would stop and point at one or another and tell me whom it had belonged to. Most were her mom's, carried over first to Hong Kong sometime in 1959, then all the way to Sacramento in 1966. Some pieces were from my dad's mom; some were wedding gifts from her brothers and aunties. My dad's wedding ring was always somewhere in the pile because he complained it was too uncomfortable to wear. Some were modern diamond pieces my mom could finally afford for herself in America. A few sweepingly romantic pendants were from my dad for an early anniversary or birthday. I knew all their rough and smooth surfaces, their dents, and the bitter, mothy smell the box exhaled each of the hundreds of times I dove in.

I stopped waiting up for my mom when I had homework to finish or a new episode of something to watch, and because we never had much to talk about. My mom spent long days cooking in my grandfather's restaurant, coming home long after nine o'clock closing to shower and collapse into bed. My dad would come up an hour later, drowsy from the television. Some nights I watched TV on her bed until she emerged from the bathroom, lotioned her swollen hands, and told me to turn it off and go to bed. The only time she would delay her lying down was if I was looking through the jewelry, and even some of those nights she would merely sigh, gather the pieces, and put them away without any stories.

By the time we were done sorting the new jewelry and beginning to peel sweet potatoes for Thanksgiving dinner, my mom had moved on from talking about gold prices to how we'd cook the turkey. I didn't ask how she had chosen which pieces to part with. But she seemed happy with her new bracelet, which gleamed as she wiped off my counters and reheated a bottle I had just made for the baby.

I started thinking about how expensive that year had been for our family. Our second daughter's birth in October left us with a fairly high bill even after insurance, and now we would have two kids in daycare after three months of unpaid maternity leave. We also needed to install new second-floor air conditioning before summer arrived. I had worried about money all year, even after we refinanced the house and switched to cheaper health insurance. I added up next year's potential tax return, the escrow return from our original home loan, a few editing job paychecks, and summer teaching paychecks. I subtracted the cost of travel to two family weddings and overnight babysitting. I tried to remind myself that no one in our family was out of work, sick, hungry, or hurting for toys. I thought of my community college students choosing between keeping their lights on or paying for post-op medication. I thought of the names of all those in need of healing listed in our church bulletin and read during the Prayer of the Faithful. I went on worrying.

My parents socked away money instead of buying nice things, and they taught me the same pride in wealth gained through self-denial. We bought only what we found on discount, and we chose only restaurants for which the *Orange County Register* ran a coupon. My parents hate both salad and potatoes, but they gobbled up the steak dinners at Sizzler on Tuesdays because that's when seniors ate for half off. My mom would look around at all the fools paying full price, pursing her lips with satisfaction. My lesson: neither your enjoyment nor your desire matter. What you enjoy is the discount. You enjoy the freedom and hope and possibility of everything you can spend the other fifty percent on. Only that spending never comes because saving money isn't a series of choices leading up to a payoff; saving money is a mindset, a mantra, and a deep fear.

It was not my parents' act of saving that I couldn't understand. It was the microsavings that never added up. We ate only free ketchup packets so we never had to buy a whole bottle from the store, set every table and cleaned every spill with misfit take-out napkins so we never had to buy paper towels, and took a fistful of KFC honey packets that we would never use because we all hated honey. None of these savings ever freed us to work less or do more. Since my mom became a lunch lady at the local elementary school, her first job outside the restaurant after my grandfather died, my parents' fridge sat full of the half-pints of nearly expired milk my mom got to take home every Friday.

My mom loved gifts more if she knew I had gotten a great deal. And she always asked. Her pride in my thrift seemed to make up for many ill-fitting shirts and sunglasses, useless bags, and flimsy gadgets. "I like anything," she assured me, combing for the brand label, and calculating any discounts she had memorized from that store's weekly ad. She clucked her tongue if she determined the cost had been too dear, and then she would wear whatever it was with guilt and *you shouldn't have* in her eyes. My mom always said she wanted "the best" for me, so I thought that's what I should give her, but I also knew "the best" did not make her happy. Making her happy wasn't about knowing what to give; it was a mysterious jackpot we sought through timing, luck, and exhaustive hunting that needed to pay out tenfold, not unlike striking gold. So I never learned, and still don't know, what my mom actually likes. And because she taught me to value a sale more than my own tastes, I never learned what something was worth *to me*.

I rationalized selling my mom's jewelry despite the pit of guilt in my gut. At least I would not use the money to buy more jewelry. I would be practical with it, paying only for things we really needed. Wasn't that better than keeping it all hidden away in the stifling dark, never to be worn or admired? In truth, I never wore anything my mom brought me. I didn't care for gold, thick jade, or ornate designs. What I loved were my simple silver engagement and wedding rings. I hardly wore anything else. But my rings had no lucky metals or stones, not like my grandmother's twenty-four-karat pendants, so pure they practically melted against your skin. I never felt her in their soft glows. I would not find her in them. When I imagined paying off all our bills and starting the new year without any debt, I told myself I wouldn't miss any of the jewelry. I probably wouldn't have to sell all of it if gold prices were as high as my mom had said. Still, I couldn't believe I was thinking about selling off my mom's heirlooms, her family's history. But then again, my mom had done it first.

—

In the movie *Coco*, which my daughters watched obsessively, souls occupy the land of the dead and can visit the living once a year as long as someone living holds them in memory. But souls die a final death, a complete obliteration, when their memory disappears from the land of the living. Maybe this is my parents' real fear—not their death but being forgotten. That they will become a forbidden, bad-luck topic just as their own parents had.

My parents dread separation. I used to think proximity was a cure, that staying near would make them feel settled and calm. But when we are together, they take hundreds of pictures, not wanting to miss a moment but indeed missing a great deal from behind the camera. By the last evening of any visit, my mom is deep in mourning. At dinner the night before her departure, she hardly talks and only takes a few sullen bites. Throughout the meal, she repeats, "See you next time," and "Over so fast." The girls look bewildered and say, "Grandma, you're not leaving until after lunch tomorrow! Want to play Uno?" We make plans for the next visit, but my mom is already gone, long before she leaves, unable to be present during our last hours together. I know she is visited by her past when she has trouble regulating her feelings. All the goodbyes she has ever said or never got to say fill the room, lacing the food and filling our stomachs with sorrow and guilt.

Because of their experienced and inherited losses, my parents want to hold onto everything. They don't trust that something let go can return, that separation is part of being together. They keep everything close, hoarded, in the dark of a jewelry safe, or in a daughter never allowed to attend sleepovers. Unhealed losses from the past mean things cannot simply flow into and out of their lives, coming and going on their own terms. Instead, everything from misplaced change to the space I needed to become myself seemed like yet another incalculable and unbearable loss. I do not fear my parents dying. Their death will not be our separation—that has already happened.

I plan to talk about my parents after their deaths, but already that idea feels like a betrayal and a bad omen. Unlike me, my daughters are used to talking about the dead. They have been to the wakes and funeral Masses of neighbors, parishioners, teachers, and friends' parents. They have seen bodies in caskets. We have tried to answer their many questions about souls, sickness, medicine, aging, and God. I offer my own experiences, church teachings, and plenty of "I don't know." Death is both normal and utterly mysterious. My father-in-law, who died just before our wedding, is vividly present when Paul or my mother-in-law recalls his love of the Chicago White Sox, his strength and gentleness, his ritual salting of every bite of every meal. Paul and his mom talk openly and fondly about my father-in-law's wake and funeral. They had both felt buoyed by everyone who came to share how they had known and loved him, who imparted love and new versions of him for the family to carry. One of our nieces, who was not yet five at the time, twirled around the funeral home, surrounded by her cousins, filled up on snacks, and wearing a lovely dress. "Grandma," she beamed, hugging my mother-in-law's legs, "this is so fun!" My mother-in-law laughed until tears came. "Yes, honey, this is fun," she replied. My girls invoke their grandfather when they wonder if he would be proud of something they've done, when they eat high-sodium foods he would have liked, when they screech and run from Paul playing the monster game their grandfather invented. They wonder why others, older and sicker than he had been, have gone on living. They wonder what is fair, what is luck, and what is fate. And they are learning that people can be together in many ways. Gone for over seventeen years now, my father-in-law crosses into the land of the living often and, I like to think, eagerly.

"Yes, there is such a thing as a good death," writes priest and psychologist Henri Nouwen. "We have to choose between clinging to life in such a way that death becomes nothing but a failure, or letting go of life in freedom so that we can be given to others as a source of hope. . . . We can act as if we are to live forever and be surprised when we don't, but we can also live with the joyful anticipation that our greatest desire to live our lives for others can be fulfilled in the way we choose to die." I know my parents cling to this life because it is filled with good, and they don't want that to end. They shun death out of loyalty to the living. But in doing so they betray both realms: living with foreboding and resistance and meeting death with acrimony.

I can no longer live in opposition to death, where there is no room for awe or mystery. Every week, I sit, stand, and kneel before the crucifix, though many Sundays, I am so distracted or resentful or eager to be somewhere else that it does not occur to me that I am worshiping beneath a symbol of execution and that our God was put to death. By earthly standards, our God lost. My faith doesn't teach that death is therefore meaningless or that the resurrection makes death any less real. Neither is death glorified nor the object of our worship. But because it is as much a part of life as birth, death too must contain joy and hope, wonder and holiness.

I have hardly contended with death. But for the blur of my emergency C-section, I have not yet stood before death or walked through it. I don't know if I will ever believe that losing a child wouldn't break you beyond repair and prove that God is heartless. In one of my favorite hymns, we sing, "In our daily living, dying, and rising, we belong to You." Maybe all I can do is gather up all my small deaths and attend to their resurrections. Maybe this is how I will learn to live with death, which is to live in full. "This is a crucial choice and we have to 'work' on that choice every day of our lives," Henri Nouwen continues. "Death does not have to be our final failure, our final defeat in the struggle of life, our unavoidable fate. If our deepest human desire is, indeed, to give ourselves to others, then we can make our death into a final gift. It is so wonderful to see how fruitful death is when it is a free gift."

~

After Thanksgiving was over and the house was quiet again, I emptied all my mom's jewelry onto our bed. A medicinal smell bloomed from the opened silk bags. I picked through the gold—heavy chains orphaned of pendants, bracelets laden with oversized coin charms, and many rings. I could hear my mom telling me this one was a gift for my dad when he was born, this one her older brother, Yee Man, gave her as a wedding gift. There was gold my grandmother had sewn into her clothes during her escape from China, all that was left after she sold most of her possessions to pay for two places on a boat to Hong Kong.

I have two gold pieces my mom had made in Chinatown when I was a baby. One is a necklace with two rows of diamonds, hooked at the ends so they fall one above the other into the shape of a crescent. She bought it because it reminded her of a mouth thrown open in laughter, though it looked to me like a glimmering hammock. The other is a bracelet of fat carved letters that spelled HAPPY. I imagined her as a new mother, calling all of this happiness to her, trying to capture it in the right design. At his little store, her favorite jeweler, Raymond, might have felt her joy and agitation as she described the pieces she wanted and watched them emerge in his sketches. He would have understood her need for them, for both the display and invocation of happiness molded into twenty-four karats. These, my mom has told me many times, were the best, most valuable pieces—you can tell by their softness, the way they become pliable when exposed to your body's heat, that they are pure. Until she passed them on to me, both stayed in her locked box.

One morning before my classes, I checked the day's gold price. I had bookmarked a handful of websites warning me against gold sharks offering cash at only scrap prices, anyone asking me to mail in my gold, and places that would not test for purity on-site. After reading a dozen online reviews and watching a few videos on their website, I decided to take my mom's gold to a jewelry shop in North County, which promised to respect its customers, regardless of their reason for selling. They provided educational articles about the difference between consigning and selling; they explained buying for resale versus buying for scrap; they linked to gold-buying websites with real-time graphs of the day's price. In not so many words, they promised not to prey on your desperation. I didn't know it at the time, but I was looking for a place with a little compassion. Though a decent-looking pawnshop sits three blocks from my house, along with a dozen jewelry stores right here in the city, I was about to drive thirty minutes to avoid any judgment because two weeks before Christmas I was bagging up my mom's treasure into a red silk bag. I stuffed in dozens of bracelets, rings, pendants, and chains. Some were pieces I had worn as a child for luck and protection, in the ears my mom pierced when I was an infant, on the soft wrists I flicked constantly as I practiced the piano. Some had a weight my muscles still haven't forgotten, that my fingers still reach to fidget when I am bored.

Eventually deciding to leave behind the happy bracelet and smiling necklace, I stuck the swollen bag of jewelry into my purse before work. Somewhere among end-of-semester meetings and running holiday errands, I figured I would find an hour for this as well. But at the end of that day, I dug the bag out and returned it to the box. Every morning for a week, I left the house with the jewelry bag, waiting for some time to open it up. I stared at my purse hanging in my office or sagging on the passenger seat, thinking how stupid it was for me to be toting around such valuables. The jewelry was with me when I wrecked our car by skidding into an intersection covered in an inch of ice. All week, I clutched my purse closely, the secret weight inside safe and silent.

—

The jewelry store was in a long strip mall northwest of the city. Huge glass display cases mazed across the vast floor. The cool lights made the gems blink and the metals glow. Another woman walked in just ahead of me, and I swore that if I had to wait my turn awkwardly in the store I would just go home. I made my way back toward some men in suits standing around. One stepped in front of me and smiled. He made eye contact and waited, without a word.

"I wanted to . . . I brought some jewelry for appraisal," I said haltingly.

I gestured to my purse to show him where, exactly, said jewelry was. I am bad at telling people what I want, couching my demands as favor requests, with apologies for the inconvenience. I have also gotten used to salespeople jumping in, reading my mind, and whisking me toward what they already know I want. I prefer to be brought offerings to accept or decline and pretend it is by free choice and startling generosity that a salesperson tries to win me over. So I hesitated, to see if this one would nod knowingly, give me a *yes I have exactly what you need* and a *right this way*.

But he waited. He looked at me, not unkindly, as if to say, *I know you haven't yet finished, so go ahead.*

"Well, so, you buy gold, right?"

He nodded and ushered me into a boxy little alcove off the side of the store, with three walls covered in thank-you notes and pictures of smiling brides and grooms. A desk cut the space in half, and I sat with my back to the store and its gleaming cases. The man in the suit inched around to his side of the desk. Between us were a scale, some paper and pens, and a box of tissues.

"Okay," he said. "Let's see what you've got."

"Wait, how exactly does this work?" I asked, not wanting to offer the first move. "Do you pay the gold price, a melt price, or resale price?" In one breath, I had just used up all my research.

"We do all of those," he replied. His voice was quiet, not the least bit eager or hurried. He started a fresh sheet in his steno pad with the date and time.

"What's your first name?" he asked. As he wrote, he passed me a form with his free hand. "Here's what we use."

At the top of the page was the price of gold that day: $1,253 per ounce of pure gold, the same number I had seen online. The chart below broke down what they would pay for twenty-two, eighteen, fourteen, and ten karats, as well as for something they could resell as is. There were no dollar signs next to the numbers.

I emptied my bag onto the table and pushed the pile toward him. He untangled the chains and laid them neatly in a row, then organized everything else into piles. With a jeweler's glass, he examined all the clasps and hooks. Then he left, returning shortly with an iPhone and a fat pen on a cord. He opened an app, plugged the devices together, and touched one of my chains with the pen's battered felt tip. Numbers flashed on the screen like a digital scale calibrating. He touched the gold over and over, looking for a good reading, adjusting his glasses as if that would help with accuracy. I watched the chains register first at eighteen, then twenty-two karats. In its fluctuations, the meter would, for a second, linger on twenty-four, but it always came down again. None of the pieces were, as my mom had told me, the most precious gold that you could only get in China fifty years ago before merchants started sneaking in other metals while still charging the same price. These were not the pure secret treasure of our family, hoarded away from the swindling American market. You could not, it seemed, tell by weight or heft or an old Chinese vendor's word what the true value was.

Slowly, the salesman made his way through all the gold, documenting each piece's purity, weight, description, and price—that last column was starting to add up to several thousand dollars. As he worked, I felt a space free up in my head. Suddenly the air conditioning project seemed less extravagant and more necessary; the car felt like a happy upgrade instead of a tragic expense. The jewelry, too, felt like a weight about to be lifted, to be given over in exchange for some breathing room. I settled into the idea that this place was not a scam operation, that their technology was not rigged against my mom's stories.

But when he said, "Oh, what a nice little ring! I like this one. We'll probably resell it as is," I changed my mind. He was admiring a ring my mom had made to house some tiny, loose diamonds saved from other broken pieces. She had chosen a modern, white gold band and a large square setting to encrust all those diamonds in tight rows. She gave it to me right after I got engaged, the same way she had given me hanging art and wedding earrings—right after she had seen what I had chosen for myself. The salesman hadn't commented on any of the jewelry until then, not the old-fashioned or mismatched gold, not the other three rings with their dulled opals and topaz. But he liked this ring which I had never worn. The thoughts appeared before I could catch myself: Someone else would buy it as is, and she would wear it not as admonition but just as a ring. I would not let her have such an easy time of owning it. As soon as he added the resale price of the ring to my payout column, I decided to leave. I was sorry to have taken up nearly an hour of his day, but he didn't know who I was, and he would still collect a paycheck. I could go home, put it all back, and give it to my daughters as I had always, if only in the abstract, intended. All that financial peace of mind slipped away.

But then I thought, maybe I could keep my newly freed mindset *and* the jewelry. It would only take a little effort on my part to have a better attitude, remember my blessings, and stop worrying about problems that didn't even exist, especially if those problems seemed so neatly erased with money. Where, I wondered, was this refreshing perspective last week when I was making yet another budget spreadsheet of school tuition we'd be paying in two and a half years? Surely a little cash in hand wouldn't suddenly balance my life and quell my anxieties. Surely I wasn't so easily bought.

Between this stranger and me, my mother's jewelry sat like a blameless pet I was about to relinquish. I had learned from a few online videos what happens to scrap gold: metallurgists take an acetylene torch to a crucible of random gold pieces. It takes several minutes for it all to melt under the blue flame. The glowing, molten gold is then poured into a bouillon mold and covered, kind of like batter in a waffle maker. In one shot, you can see air bubbles escaping, popping out bright orange like some liquid night sky. The new gold bar takes only a minute to harden, then is plunged into water that instantly turns boiling. Any debris is chiseled away. I knew this would be—though with far less ceremony than even a YouTube video—the fate of my mom's pieces: strewn with various strangers' grit and body oil and happiness, reduced to something pure at last.

But I didn't ask for my jewelry back. I stayed in my seat and let the salesman, now misted in sweat from our hour in his suit, finish his tally and present me with a final total of just over four thousand dollars. Whether inertia propelled me to hand over my driver's license, or the taste of a minute's freedom from worry allowed me to sign the sales agreement, I'm not entirely sure. When he left to print my check, my nose stung as if I had been punched, and my face crumpled. I shook out a tissue and heaved into the already dissolving square. The spasm in my chest and the drum in my sinuses felt like some kind of assault from the outside. I could not release the contortion of my face or my shoulders. My whole body was surging with regret, betrayal, embarrassment, and some other kind of ache. These pieces had touched my ancestors' skin. They held the shape of our history in their castings. I didn't want to sell them, but I didn't want the jewelry. I wanted to hear my mom tell stories again, but I didn't want to be waiting up alone for the chance of a conversation with her. I wanted so many things from my mom instead of old jewelry every time she visited. In these burnished piles, I was carrying all of my parents' fears and refusals and denial. I needed to set them down but I couldn't help mourning the death of their current forms.

Despite my sobbing, I thought to put on my coat so I could dash out of the store the minute we finished. But I was blowing my nose, and so didn't hear the salesman return with my check and all the jewelry neatly gathered on a numbered tray.

"Oh," he said. "Miss."

"I'm sorry." I turned away my leaking face.

"I was just going to show you this sheet," he said gently. "This says you have seven days to change your mind." He counted on his fingers: seven business days meant I had until next Thursday to return.

"You would give me everything back? After all that work?"

"You have to come back with our check first," he chuckled. "And then yes, we'll give it all back. People change their minds all the time. Seven days. It's the law."

On their testimonials page, one customer thanked the store for her granddaughter's breathing machine, another for a month of food after his workman's comp payout had ended. People thanked Leo, Chris, and Charlie for their kindness. I wondered which one of them was my salesman, why he had never said his name, why I'd never thought to ask. I folded the check into my purse, still sniffling. The jewelry lay like a collection of spiny little sea creatures.

"Are you sure you're all right?" he asked.

"Yes, I'm fine," I said. "I'm sorry."

"It's okay. I know those pieces meant something to you."

A small laugh escaped as I put my empty red bag into my purse and snapped it shut. But then I nodded. I smiled at his kindness and shook his hand.

"They did," I said.

One of my recurring fantasies is cleaning out my parents' overstuffed house. I dream of the dumpsters I will fill with wobbly discount lamps, endless logo-branded blankets, and sample-sized cereals. Room by room, I gut the house to its corners and unburden it from decades-old paint, dot matrix printers, and VHS tapes. I open every window and can almost feel the house float away on the Santa Ana winds. I have been having this same daydream since I was a teenager.

I grew up in a room half full of my dad's old stuff. Among the relics: a never-assembled model human digestive system, an unstrung guitar, and every toy ever won at a raffle, carnival game, or fishbowl drawing. Prizes, no matter how cheap or useless, were emblems of prosperity. A four-foot-tall plush and menacing Pink Panther lurked in my closet, by far the biggest we had ever won from some Las Vegas arcade. As I packed for college, I found my mom removing all the "valuables" from a donation bag I had stuffed with toys and outgrown clothes. My parents imbued objects, whether extra condiments or heirloom jewelry, with the power to capture fortune and cast it into our futures. If we won candy or a bottle of wine, we could not spoil its charm by consuming it. Around us, they rooted down free stuff like the poles of an electric fence, inside of which we lived in a mausoleum of ourselves chasing after every scrap of luck and happiness and bounty.

With the check in hand, I was suddenly afraid the jewelry had become just another thing I needed to get rid of for the sake of annihilating clutter. Had I been unable to grasp its value because all I see in my parents' things is fear and defense against the unknown? I let the seven-day return deadline pass before I deposited the check. After a few more days, I finally took the empty jewelry bag out of my purse and dropped it into an always-growing donation bin in the basement. That spring, we installed the new air conditioning and have spent many nights rocking our girls under its impressive breeze. I think of how my mom would *tsk* because, rather than solicit bids, we just picked a local company to install the unit. I think, each time

I wipe my sleeping girls' sweaty brows and click on the cooling hum, each time I shop without coupons, and each time I force myself not to order the cheapest item on the menu, how extravagant my mom finds my life, how it grieves her that we, again and again, let the world get one over on us. I still worry about our spending and saving. Sometimes I count the number of things I could buy or pay off with the jewelry that is still with me, all that happiness sitting in the dark.

I haven't yet told my mom about the jewelry I sold. I don't know if she'll ever ask, or whether I'll explain that it was she who gave me the idea in the first place, that I sold it because I had wished for it to be a blessing and not a burden. The jewelry had never felt freely given or accepted, only stashed with me along with two generations of grief and scarcity. The pieces I've let go of will never drip from my daughters' hands. Someday, perhaps, they'll sort through the remainders, select what they want, and leave the rest without abandoning the dead or the living. We will share the freedom to choose what becomes ours.

On her next visit, my mom will bring more jewelry, carried on the plane inside a vitamin bottle. Her relief when I take it will be obvious, these charms and talismans now charged with protecting my family thousands of miles from her. Because I am not afraid, I don't wear her pendants like armor. I let my good fortune walk around in the bodies of my husband and daughters. My store of treasures are outgrown sleep sacks, a box of Paul's cards and letters, and a shelf of odd snow globes we collect for each other—all things I love because I love how we have lived with them, how they have held some of our greatest risks. The collection of our moments, some so sweet I can hardly form the words for them, is starting to outgrow the many other stockpiles we keep. I am stashing away the furtive delight of walking out to dinner after both of us had promised, then forgotten, to defrost something. I am storing up each taste of the immoderate number of dishes we order, and the chain of our grubby hands sustaining the endless grace we say. Losing any of this would be worse than being separated by death. I have loved that in our life, we have been caught unprepared, we have overpaid and underbought, we have taken our luck when it came, and then we have let it go.

INITIATIONS

When we returned in May 2015 from a semester of living abroad, my husband and I were imbued with a new sense of commitment and gratitude for where we lived. I was never so glad for our little brick house, our neighborhood, and our shrinking parish as when we came back from Madrid. Even the St. Louis humidity felt like a gift. Our time in Madrid had been glorious—the rich food, daily life centered around public spaces, a culture that valued leisure. But we felt returned to ourselves in our city, in our church, among the routines and people we loved. At our first Mass after arriving home, the liturgy settled me like a newborn in a swaddle. I found calm in the music, the priest's unvarying intonations, the worn pews and squeaky kneelers. I hadn't realized how unsettled I had been. In the spirit of our renewed commitment, we decided it was time to baptize our girls.

Part of me wanted to wait until I was myself was baptized, but I had no idea when that would be. I worried about scheduling their initiations before mine. What kind of a guide would that make me? Our pastoral associate, Sr. M, had warned me I should not wait too long for their sacraments. If my oldest turned seven unbaptized, she would have to go through the same year-long process of entering the church as an adult convert. When I told a friend about my hesitations, she said she wasn't raising her kids with any religion because they should be free to choose for themselves. I thought about her choice and later realized my friend and I wanted the same things for our kids. Baptizing our girls wouldn't take away our daughters' choice. It would give them something *to* choose instead of leaving them to do all the seeking on their own. We wanted our girls to have life in the church fully available to them since this was the spiritual home we were offering. Which meant receiving a sacrament they didn't yet understand or choose for themselves. They could choose later, of course, not to stay. They could certainly become alienated, angry, or indifferent, or find another faith. If they did, at least they would know exactly what they were rejecting. We scheduled their baptism for September.

For Catholics, baptism, confirmation, and the Eucharist (Communion) are the sacraments of initiation, through which you become a member of the church. Those who are born and raised in the church receive all three by the time they are in middle school. Those like me, who join later, undergo the Rite of Christian Initiation of Adults (RCIA). *Initiation* conjures an ancient, tribal world. In our culture that prizes individualism, *initiation* gets saddled with negative, painful, and even humiliating associations. The word connotes cliques, cults, gangs, hazing, being broken down and brought low before we can belong. Usually, there is some gatekeeper deciding whether you are accepted or outcast. These negative and nearly all-male connotations colored my view of RCIA.

The writer Michael Meade calls anything like this a "deteriorated" form of initiation, carried out because society's elders have failed to show young people what real, communal, life-giving initiation should be. Meade defines initiation as stepping into a new self, which "requires that aspects of the old sense of identity be sacrificed and left behind," and which involves a process of "entering life, facing death in some form, and finding renewal." His archetype of initiation has three stages: "First, some event separates us from what is familiar; then, some struggle or ordeal ensues. If we survive, we return with new knowledge and a greater sense of life." Separation-ordeal-return is Meade's basic structure of how we gain knowledge and move into a new phase of life. Initiations, he writes, were how societies "consciously assisted and enhanced life's essential patterns of change." Meade continues, "Rites of initiation were created to interrupt a person's life and arrest their vision, to stop their habitual ways of seeing life and open the psyche to a greater view of the world and their place in it."

I knew separation and ordeal but never return. My elders, because they were denied meaningful initiations themselves and because they were torn from their culture and not fluent in America's, did not hold rites of passage for my generation. My family's immigration is a kind of incomplete initiation—unending separation compounded with the absence of a society to return to. Meade describes what happens when initiation is begun but left unfinished: "what could have changed a person altogether and revealed something essential in their life becomes buried in the shadowy areas of the psyche. . . . There remains an incompleteness, a sense that something could have happened but did not." I saw this incompleteness, this languishing and melancholy, in both my parents and my grandfather, in the way they kept isolated from community and were at a loss to help the next generations create new selves.

For one, my grandfather never left the restaurant, except to pick up supplies in Chinatown on Wednesdays. When I was small and spending all my days at the restaurant, I sometimes tagged along in our wood-paneled station wagon, crammed between crates of celery and boxes of thirty dozen eggs. But for the exceptionally rare occasions we would stop at McDonald's after a long afternoon of shopping, it was always a given that he did not eat in other people's restaurants. In one watery memory, my grandfather, in dark, grease-stained corduroy pants and a plaid button-down shirt, unwraps a Big Mac while I drench Chicken McNuggets in barbeque sauce. No words ever pass between us, but I do remember him eating away the dry edges of his burger until a perfect, juicy, crustless bite juts from the center like a jigsaw piece, which he offers to me. It crunches with pickle and onion, but I finish it with obedience and awe.

Birthdays, anniversaries, graduations, and holidays passed, and we knew my grandfather would not acknowledge them or attend the occasional small gathering. Once, when my parents' car broke down at the restaurant, my grandfather drove us home after closing, and I was shocked to learn that he knew the way. He didn't come in, and he never traveled to our home again. I think about him landing in a new country at age twelve, right when one would expect several initiations into manhood to begin. But he'd had no mentors or even caregivers as he drifted among Chinatown restaurant backdoors, scraping by on leftovers and sheer will. How disoriented he must have been, and must have stayed, even past finding that first shelter, food, and fitful sleep. Despite years of trauma and isolation, my grandfather learned to cook, got married, and had four children, for whom he provided a comfortable life, but in whose American lives he did not participate. All four graduated from high school (three from college, one with an advanced degree, and one with military service), married, and had children themselves. My grandfather trusted others to help the next generation navigate systems of education, work, and government.

My parents likewise deferred to the authority of my school, piano teachers, coaches, and driver's ed instructors. They depended on other Americans to lead me across thresholds, from one stage of life to another, because they did not feel fully part of the culture themselves. Despite their trust and dependence on others for my American education, they bristled at the changes brought on. For initiation doesn't just change the individual who is separated and returned; it calls for a shift in the whole community, which must, Meade writes, "truly recognize the changes and offer healing" so the initiated one is "welcomed back as a changed person with new knowledge of both life and death." The interruption and change of a proper initiation precede one's return to the society from which one was temporarily separated. But what about a life interrupted, not by ritual, but by war, famine, and exile? What about a life after immigration that remains a permanent interruption? My family did not change with me. Having endured so much upheaval and loss, they clung to the familiar, to steadiness and routine—from which deviations felt like a betrayal. The roles of children and parents weren't meant to evolve. Children should remain deferential, obedient, and nearby, while parents remain financially supportive decision-makers. When roles remain locked, Michael Meade cautions, "the loss of meaningful rites of passage often leaves an ambivalence between parents and children, as childhood has no clear ending." Even after college, marriage, and babies of our own, at no point are children seen as fellow adults, but continue to live a half-life of adulthood under parental expectations, influence, pressure, and financial support. The idea that parents would partake in, let alone celebrate, their children belonging more fully to the world was absurd.

And so, I marked milestones outside my family. I hosted my own college graduation party, inviting most of my mom's Sacramento family—her two brothers, one sister, and all their spouses, children, and grandchildren, along with several of my friends. Unfamiliar with the city I had been living in for the past four years, as they only ever came to drop me off and bring me home for the first summer, my parents left the planning to me. Four years before, I had arranged my high school graduation party for my dad's much smaller family. Dinner had been at the Chinese restaurant near our house, where we gathered for almost every occasion, and everyone had felt comfortable and casual. At my university's convocation for English majors, everyone looked august in their regalia. Every name called rang with possibility. From the stage, draped in a beautiful blue-and-white lei my friend in the stands had bought for me, I felt myself passing through a door held open by our professors, changed and ready to be sent forth. I worried that my family was uncomfortable on the outdoor cement stadium seating, but mostly I surged with the thrill of leaving to buy my first car, move to New Mexico, and start graduate school.

I found everyone after the ceremony, and we stood in the shade for pictures before heading to dinner at a Chinese restaurant I had chosen, a twenty-minute drive across two freeways. I could only explain that because parking was a nightmare in Berkeley, I had chosen a restaurant in an East Bay strip mall with a huge lot. As we walked across the parking lot, my mom said, "I don't see everyone. Why is this place so far? Maybe people got lost." We all had cell phones, and everyone found their way eventually. Our group took up four tables, immediate families together, me with my friends. The flavors were a little different from what we were used to; our favorite eggplant in garlic sauce and shrimp and walnuts tasted heavier and sweeter here.

A few minutes into the meal, my mom crouched over my chair. "There isn't enough food," she whispered sharply.

Agitated, she gestured to the tables. Plates were emptying fast, some already scraped clean. Soda cups sat drained. But people were talking and laughing and taking pictures.

"I thought I ordered enough," I said, my teeth gritted.

"You know your cousins all have big appetites! You should have ordered more. People are *hungry*."

"No, I didn't know that," I snapped, thrusting my chair back. "I'll get some more," I muttered.

I ordered each table three more dishes plus white rice, aflame with embarrassment and envy of all my friends who had parties waiting for them at home or in restaurants where their parents had made reservations and were probably giving toasts. Furious and alone, I wished to be invited to my celebration instead of overseeing it. *I should have known* churned in me. But I didn't know my cousins on my mom's side, or their eating habits. It shouldn't have been my job to guess. And the dinner hadn't been for them. But my cousins, who graciously and gratefully polished off the extra dishes, had never said a word about the food. They pressed cards with generous checks into my hands and politely accepted the leftovers.

My parents had been anxious witnesses at every one of my initiations, big or small. Through no fault of their own, they had missed walking across their own thresholds and so could not meet me on the other side of mine. How could they welcome me into a society that didn't always see them as full or legitimate members? To complete an initiation, Michael Meade concludes, "a small death must come between parents and their child. . . . Something of the entanglement between parents and child must die in order for the tree of life to continue to grow." But for parents with immigration trauma, who already lived separated from themselves and society, any kind of loss is intolerable, even if imperative for growth and thriving, even if it meant the birth of something more vibrant and lasting.

Physician and writer Rachel Naomi Remen recalls in her essay collection *My Grandfather's Blessings*, "I believe I know the very moment that I became an adult, when my relationship to my mother as a child was complete." In Remen's long career as a doctor, counselor, and speaker, she had not invited her mother to one of her lectures until nearly the end of her mother's life. Speaking to a full auditorium with her mother present for the first time, Remen noticed that "suddenly people began to applaud and slowly many even stood up. Only one person in the tenth row remained seated. Her arms were crossed and there was a very tiny smile on her face. As we continued to look at each other, her eyes narrowed and she nodded, slowly, twice. No other acknowledgment I have ever received has equaled it." Her mother's acknowledgment was, to be sure, of Remen's accomplishment, but it was also of her belonging to this crowd, to her patients, to her vocation. Her mother's nod, which brought childhood to a close at last, was approval, admiration, and to say, *I am sharing you now.*

After the last graduation guests had gone, my parents and I headed to collect my things from the dorm. The next day, we would drive six hours to their home, where I would promptly pack again and head eight hundred miles east in the Jeep Wrangler I had planned to buy from the used car dealership near my grandfather's restaurant. I'm not sure when I mentioned finally saving enough for a down payment on my dream car, but when we arrived at their house, the white Volvo sedan that they had picked out for me was waiting in the driveway. When they handed me the thick key fob, they said, "A safe car. Safer than most." I would drive it toward the high desert, far away and indeed safe within its compact frame.

Since I've lived apart from them, my parents have presented me with many more things to replace what I already had: a pressure cooker; a blender; cleaning supplies; art; a jewelry box. In recent years, they have offered to install a doorbell security system because they hear crime is rising in my city, and solar panels on our roof to offset the increased cooling they believe our daughters need to be comfortable upstairs. I know they just want to feel useful, that without the markers of their old role, they feel unmoored. I know their only framework for being in my life is as the parents of a child. But when every initiation stands contrary to their idea of filial piety, my only choices feel like stay or go, belong or don't. Unable to support or participate in my initiation hungers, my parents have given me what they can in objects they think I need to be an adult.

———

The urgency for my own sacraments arose as soon as Paul and I decided to baptize our daughters. I wanted to have at least *something* figured out before I initiated them into our faith. But, despite a lifetime of initiation hunger, I didn't want to go through RCIA, not according to the program our pastoral associate, Sr. M, insisted on. Something about the rigidity, from the start date to holding precisely six inquiry sessions, to the Easter Vigil being the only day I could receive the sacraments, felt amiss, exactly opposite to the calm and settledness I felt at Mass. I kept going every week and I read feverishly that summer—Scripture, Pope Francis, theology, spiritual reflections. I signed up for an eleven-week Bible study, and I attended a day-long retreat. But the new fall semester was fast approaching, and I was nowhere near closer to an answer. I didn't know what I wanted. I didn't know why I didn't know.

"You sound like," Paul offered, "you could use a spiritual director." I was uneasy about sharing my doubts and hesitations about RCIA with a priest, but he told me spiritual directors can be women, religious, or laypeople. When Paul briefly considered joining a religious order, he was told to find a spiritual director and do some serious discernment work about his desires, motivations, and life situation. "They help you listen for God and discern," he said. "They wouldn't push you one way or another about baptism, or any decision, but just help you figure out what you really want." The idea filled me with relief, even consolation. I was grateful for Paul's knowledge and suggestion, and for the new project of finding a spiritual director.

I found a directory on the Aquinas Institute of Theology's website. The institute, a Dominican graduate school in theology and ministry, kept a list of active directors who specialized in discernment, grief, addiction, recovery, and many other areas. I chose Sr. V because her listed address was five minutes from home. A vowed religious sister also appealed to me because she would be someone who had made a choice and commitment. In response to my email, she wrote that she was open to new directees, but she had moved to her order's home about thirty minutes south. Her email contained an inordinate number of exclamation points. But her response had been quick and enthusiastic. The inner *yes* I was learning to listen to signaled. I realized it had always been with me, a quiet, firm kind of whisper: *this*. I rearranged my office hours on Sr. V's first available day, which was three days before my girls' baptism.

Sr. V's home, a former Boy Scout lodge tucked behind a cemetery, housed the order of sisters she belonged to. I had no framework for spiritual direction, so I used what I was familiar with: school. I headed into my first meeting ready to study my way to an answer about baptism. Sr. V, I decided, would help me make a well-informed decision. I arrived at our first meeting promptly, in slacks and a blazer, straight from teaching. She came to the door before I rang the bell, in a modern white habit, knee-length and short-sleeved. A black headpiece trimmed in white revealed a few inches of sandy hair. Her smile was broad and she said, "Well, hello there!" with her hands on her hips, as if she'd spent the day impatient over my arrival. I offered a handshake, and she took it, looking entirely amused. She released my hand but didn't move.

"I'm just," she said, scrunching up her shoulders, "going to give you a little hug."

I laughed and accepted, immediately disarmed.

After a tour of the house, we settled into plush cobalt rockers in the living room. I told her about my family and work, how I had come to the church and my husband had returned. I framed my seeking as a question of whether I could abide by the church's teachings, whether I could tolerate the RCIA process. Receiving the sacraments was posed as an intellectual problem about rule following. No high stakes. No risk of heartbreak. Sr. V listened intently. She offered no workaround to my problem, no quick way to make peace with the church's rules.

"Let's start with what you want at this moment," she said. "God speaks to us through our desires. It's then that we have to discern God's voice from all the other voices, all the noise."

"I don't know what I want," I replied, which felt dreadful and freeing to say.

In my family, denying your desires showed deference, loyalty, and sacrifice. "Doesn't matter to me" and "anything is fine" were my parents' answers to every question. They staunchly refused to impose themselves on anyone. Except of course they did, with hints about "what's best" or declarations about what so-and-so *needs*. The way we chose where to eat out on my mom's day off was for my dad to say, "Mom hasn't had a burger in a long time. . . ." or for my mom to offer, "The place with the salad bar is healthy for Dad. . . ." I, then, couldn't dare suggest otherwise without undermining these demonstrations of care. Their roles would be fulfilled, one sacrificing and the other absolved of any want. It always left me guessing and unable to receive anything without the shame of someone else's self-denial, which still sometimes paralyzes me. But telling Sr. V "I don't know" was a relief. It was the reason I had come. I wasn't letting her down by not having an answer.

I continued, "Until recently, I'd been fine with the way things were. I was part of the parish. I didn't feel like anything was missing. Then, the way to get baptized became an obstacle for me. I can't actually tell if it's something I desire, or if it's just that I'm mad because I was told *no*."

I explained what Sr. M had said about my not being included in the Liturgy of the Eucharist, and that the RCIA timeline and requirements were my only option for baptism. I held my breath, afraid that Sr. V would agree, which would mean taking Sr. M's side. Instead, Sr. V rolled her eyes and groaned.

"Okay, well, yes," she sighed. "The church does teach that the baptized are invited to the Eucharist." Turning very serious, she continued, "But the Holy Spirit and the incarnation of Christ are present *to us all.*"

I had needed this affirmation more than I realized, for that familiar Catholic refrain, "all are welcome," to feel true, as it had when the priest at that college Mass had waved and winked to include us all.

"So then," Sr. V noted, "you weren't told *no* about your baptism, exactly?"

"I guess?" I stammered.

"Well, you were told there is one way to do RCIA at your parish."

"Right."

"Could you find another parish? Another priest who might be willing to work with you?"

"I've probably already missed the window to start RCIA this year too," I sighed, before I caught what her question implied. "Wait, are you saying that I can get baptized without going through RCIA?"

"People do it all the time," Sr. V replied. My mouth must have dropped because she emphasized, "You *do not* have to do RCIA in order to be baptized. The process exists for a reason, and there are many benefits to completing it. But it's not the only way."

I never imagined variation in the process, that I could have just asked our pastor, or a Jesuit friend, or anyone for, essentially, a second opinion. How was I to know that Sr. M's insistence had been for her way and not the only way? Fresh anger burned behind my eyes. For not being shown, or entrusted with, the whole picture. For not knowing, yet again, what I didn't know.

Sr. V waited while I wrangled my feelings. It would be a while before I allowed myself to process them with her instead of believing I needed to get ahold of myself before we could talk.

"I don't know when I'll be ready, but I do want to be baptized in my parish," I said eventually. "I guess it means I'll have to wait some more."

"There's plenty to discern in the meantime." Sr. V smiled.

"Well, I may not know about me yet, but my daughters are getting baptized this Saturday," I shared.

"Congratulations! What a blessing." Sr. V glowed.

"I feel like I should be better prepared as their mom."

"They're how old?"

"Four and almost two," I replied, laughing at her arched eyebrows. "I know they're not going to be asking me big theological questions just yet. But I feel like I should be doing more than just . . . throwing a party."

"A party is *exactly* what this should be. You will all grow in your understanding of baptism together. But for now, this is a big reason to celebrate."

I felt okay for the first time in a year. Stuck, unsure, angry, and okay. I didn't know why a door still felt shut when I thought about my own baptism, but I no longer needed to kick it in. I felt softer somehow, almost ready, as the French Jesuit Pierre Teilhard de Chardin advised, to "accept the anxiety of feeling yourself in suspense and incomplete."

Sr. V smiled broadly. "You know this is wonderful news, right? You're baptizing your daughters out of love. Whatever decision you make for yourself, it will be out of love, too."

Three days later, on a warm September Saturday, my girls were baptized in our church by Paul's friend and former teacher from his Jesuit high school. I was aware that most baptisms happened during Sunday Mass, so the parish could reflect on their own first sacrament. At the time, we still knew more people outside the parish than in and wanted to be surrounded by those who had known us the longest. I went to the secondhand clothing store to pick out white dresses that could be happily wrecked by the end of the day. We held our daughters over the font while they scissor-kicked and tried to wriggle out from under the stream of water but never cried. Their godparents, two of Paul's brothers and their wives, lit their baptism candles and promised to walk with us all in this new light. The bittersweet spice of chrism, the consecrated anointing oil, lasted all day, and I sniffed their foreheads every chance I got. We catered a picnic in the park with fried chicken and an enormous cake. Paul's family and my parents came, along with parish friends, the beloved women of our daycare, and colleagues from both our schools who had known us for years before our turn to the church. A feeling of fullness, which I experienced during Mass when the right elixir of sleep, morning light on the stained glass, hymns, and gratitude opened me to the Spirit and people all around, enveloped our little party that afternoon. We could not, would not have wanted, to initiate our girls without this family of witnesses, not all worshippers nor baptized, but each one a holy story within ours. Unlike my eldest's red egg party, I did not ask anyone else to plan the ceremony. Paul and I stood with our girls before their sacrament and, along with our community, received them afterward.

That night, we tucked away their candles, each bearing the smallest indent in the wax from their first soft minutes of light.

—

Two weeks after my daughters' baptism, Paul and I flew to Albuquerque for a cousin's wedding, leaving our girls with my mother-in-law as we escaped for a long weekend to revisit our old graduate school haunts. We went to Friday night Mass at the Cathedral of St. Francis of Assisi, a pale stone basilica near the main plaza in Santa Fe, glowing in warm uplighting and a watermelon sunset of late September. Mass felt new and strange under these plaster arches and images of the Virgin of Guadalupe. I felt outside myself. The unfamiliarity was enough for me to turn to Paul and say, "I think I want to go up for Communion."

He smiled. "That's great," he whispered beside me. "You should go."

"Do you think anyone will know I'm not supposed to?"

"Maybe when the lightning and thunder start," he quipped.

"All right, all right," I hissed as I stood to follow the others in our pew toward the aisle.

I kept an arm's length behind the woman in front of me, my hands folded as I had seen others do on countless Sundays in St. Louis. I made a small bow before the host and cupped my hands together. The man distributing Communion on our side of the church held up a perfectly round, almost translucent wafer with the faintest imprint of a cross in the middle.

"The Body of Christ," he said as he placed it in my hands.

"Amen," I replied and brought it to my tongue.

I stepped over to the woman holding a metal chalice. "The Blood of Christ," she said as she wiped the rim from the previous person, then rotated to a fresh spot for me.

"Amen," I said as I touched the wine to my lips, terrified that I would backwash into the vessel. The sharp fumes barely registered on my tongue. I headed back to our pew, remembering to make the sign of the cross a little more than halfway back. Paul kept pace behind me, and we settled into our kneelers while the rest of the packed church filed up to receive and return to their kneelers. I watched them intently, tourists in cargo shorts and fanny packs, older women with black lace veils covering their hair, parents and children, Latino and white, awkward fumblers and practiced faithful. I was folded into the crowd, my secret on exactly no one's mind, including God's. The host wasn't dissolving, so I pressed it to the roof of my mouth and felt it snap in two. I rolled it around, trying to name its flavor, but it was like tasting the air, and then it was gone.

"How does it feel?" Paul asked after the final note of the closing song.

"It feels . . . fine," I said. "But are you sure that wasn't just a terrible idea?"

"I don't think anyone's going to be upset that you wanted to receive the Eucharist. I bet you half the people in here tonight, including us, aren't in a state of grace the way the church means it. And who better to receive?"

Something did feel different as I walked out of the cathedral, the thin and crisp Santa Fe air somehow more receptive to light. Paul and I hadn't been away or alone for this long since our two-year-old was born, and we savored the hour-long drive back to Albuquerque. Maybe the spark was from our getaway or the nostalgia of our first city together, or the warm char of roasting green chiles in the autumn air. Maybe it was all a form of saying *yes* and receiving.

⁓

Two weeks after my illicit Communion, Sr. M and our pastor announced that they were leaving the parish. Fr. J was being reassigned to another parish, which happened routinely after seven years or so. He had been at our parish for ten. And Sr. M was being called back to her order's main headquarters in another state. The pews echoed with gasps and sighs, bodies shifting and heads shaking. As all the news settled, something in me shifted, just a little.

By early November, the new pastor, Fr. P, arrived. I wondered if he would require RCIA in the same way as Sr. M. I wondered why, suddenly, the program didn't seem quite as onerous as it had just a month ago. I kept meaning to ask about it, but then it was Thanksgiving, and I still hadn't made an appointment. I wasn't wrestling with whether I should. I *wanted* to ask about baptism. I was hopeful I would be ready to move forward. And that hope was stirring up a restlessness, maybe even a hunger. But I wasn't asking. I wasn't doing the thing I wanted, and my ambivalence unnerved me.

When I told Sr. V the news about our personnel changes, she nodded slowly. "It sounds like," she said with a slight smile, "God has opened a door for you."

For two years, I had been looking for God, never in that time thinking God was with me. I had felt alone in my waiting and my resistance. Her words felt true and right, but also deeply unsettling. What was I doing looking for something that was already with me? What was I wrestling so hard with if the object of my seeking was already mine?

"Yes," I replied, taking in the idea.

Spiritual direction, among other things, helps you see where God is present in your life and where God is calling you. When that felt too uncomfortable, I resorted to asking a lot of graduate seminar questions about the inconsistencies of the Bible or the dehumanizing aspects of church teachings about birth control, gay marriage, women's exclusion, and abortion. I wanted answers. I wanted belonging to the church to make sense. Sr. V welcomed my scrutiny but always turned the conversation back to my experience of God. What was God saying to me with this question? Where is God *in* the question? What was I saying to God about it?

"Maybe," she continued, "you're not looking for God so much as how to have a relationship with God."

"That's it," I agreed. It was a relationship I both sought and avoided. I would have to rely on my own desire to answer this call. All I knew was that I didn't want to feel alone in my desire. I wanted to be wanted in return.

"I don't know who I am, who either of us is, in the relationship. I think it's the metaphors—servant, slave, wheat, lamb, lost coin, child. They don't . . . work for me."

The poet and essayist Kathleen Norris writes, "For reasons I did not comprehend, church seemed a place I needed to be." In turning toward faith, she needed a new language. "But in order to inhabit it, to claim it as mine, I had to rebuild my religious vocabulary. The words had to become real to me in an existential sense." For me, it was the metaphor of being found and returned, the implication that I had spent my life being lost. And then there was my overwhelming sense of betrayal.

I told Sr. V that my parents felt like the biggest obstacle in my conversion. Not at all because they disapproved of my new faith. They were, if anything, indifferent to it.

"Everything my faith tells me to do is the opposite of what my parents taught me—about money, death, desire, strangers, time, adoption, vulnerability. Everything I'm asked to say yes to feels like a rejection, even a rebuke of them."

"God would never ask you to turn away from anyone or your past," she replied. "Jesus asks us to follow Him. We might have to walk away from some things to do that. But we're also commanded to love."

"Sometimes I wonder if I am doing all this *because* it's in opposition to the way I was raised. That my seeking is a *no* and not a *yes*."

"God is not either-or," she replied. "God is far too expansive for that."

"I just don't feel like there is room for both."

"You don't have to choose one over the other. You can't, actually. It's all one—it's all your life." After a pause, she added, "You can say no to the things you were taught without saying no to the people who taught you."

It was reassurance and permission I didn't know I needed. My parents and I were not estranged exactly, but our lives were not what I would have called shared. I had not sought them out in a long time. Even so, this initiation felt charged in a way none other had before. The very idea of conversion felt like a confrontation, but with nothing actually standing in my way, what had I been pushing against? Michael Meade might say the answer was myself. "Initiation intends to awaken the whole person," Meade writes, "especially the rejected and unknown aspects of oneself. Often the rejected, lowly parts of a person become the only way to survive and the key to growth." An entire drama was playing out within me, who first learned to say no to what I wanted, and later to what they wanted. At thirty-five years old, my desire remained rejected and somehow still tangled up with quietly resisting parental expectations. Conversion was calling me to declare and submit to my desire. But first, it would need to be rescued and resurrected.

I didn't know how any of that would happen, but something broke free enough for me to email Fr. P right after the new year. He answered right away. The first thing he wrote back was that I could be baptized anytime, that there was no rule about receiving the sacraments at Easter or prescriptively sticking to the RCIA calendar. "But," he wrote, "it would be good to start with a series of inquiry sessions." He gave me the names of two women in the parish who usually led these sessions. I emailed them next, bristling less and less against asking for what I wanted, asking for people's time, asking to be met. They, too, said *yes, let's meet*. Inquiry sessions would be on Tuesday nights during the season of Lent, which began in the bitter dark of February and lasted six weeks, through the slowly lengthening days and the first signs of spring, and ending with the holy days of Easter.

—

A combination of the holidays, the new school semester, and a family chain of colds and flu kept me from meeting with Sr. V again until April. She asked how all my inquiry meetings had been going. My girls were going through a spell of disrupted sleep, and I was afraid my bleariness was clouding the experience.

"It's not been great," I admitted, then blurted out the rest in one breath. "There are supposed to be six meetings, and we've had four so far, but all we've talked about is the liturgical calendar. I bring my Bible, but we never talk about Scripture. They haven't even asked me to share my story. When I said I struggled with prayer, they told me to pray while I washed dishes. I don't think I can do another two meetings."

I continued about how I had asked, after the first two meetings in which I didn't speak at all, if I could have some time to ask questions, which I had thought was the purpose of my inquiry. How in response to my many hesitations about joining the church they told me, the convert, how grateful and relieved they were to have been raised in faithful households because it meant they didn't struggle with doubt and so many questions. How they had told me faith was a gift I needed to pray for. And how, when I had brought up my interest in Ignatian spirituality of examining our desires as a way God speaks to us, one of them told me that theology didn't speak to her and so wouldn't be part of our meetings. And how, after criticizing the "ancient" songs played at our Mass, they advised me to listen to the local Christian rock radio station more.

Sr. V dropped her head into her hands and made a growling sound. "I'm sorry," she said, shaking her head. "That is just so very bad."

"Thanks for saying that. I thought I was losing my mind."

"You're not crazy," she assured me. "So, where are things now?"

I told her that I had been ready to quit, to walk away from all of it and just be an unbaptized person who happens to go to Mass every week. But then, one Sunday, Fr. P approached me as we were all putting on our coats and getting ready to leave.

"You're the one doing the inquiry sessions?" he asked, reaching over a pew to shake my hand.

"Yes," I replied, tempted to add, *but not for much longer.*

He nodded. "How," he began, then paused, looking for the right words. He finally sighed and shot me a very sympathetic, almost apologetic, look and said, "How can I help you with that?"

Sr. V snorted. "He knew!"

"I think so," I said. "He offered to meet with me one-on-one, instead of finishing all six meetings."

"Oh, praise God," she exclaimed.

Fr. P had told me that he'd trusted the women to run the inquiry sessions, as they had for several years before he had arrived. But after he chatted with them about the meetings and how things were going with me, he'd decided to approach me.

"It feels so hard sometimes," I admitted to Sr. V. "I'm sorry, I don't mean to moan about it. But sometimes it feels like I'm either being turned away outright or being driven away."

"But you stay," she noted, raising her eyebrows. "In the church and your parish."

"It's just stubbornness," I replied. "I mean, why should *I* leave?"

"Why else do you stay?"

She was looking for something affirmative. Not just more pushing against, not just stubborn resisting.

"Maybe the music?" I said, half embarrassed by my answer.

"Good!" she cried. "Honestly, that's the reason a lot of people stay."

"It's the people, too," I added. "How we show up together and for each other and our neighbors. It's the people, their presence and goodwill. It does mean something to me."

"Parish life is how God teaches us that we belong to each other. Even to the people we can't stand and who can't stand us."

"Do you feel that way about the sisters in your order?" I asked, astonished at the thought.

Sr. V laughed, throwing up her hands. "Only all the time! As they feel about me. But you keep showing up, right? Because I think you know we cannot have faith without others. It's why you haven't changed parishes and why you keep waiting out your obstacles."

Ronald Rolheiser names community as a nonnegotiable element in the spiritual life. Without community, he writes, one lacks a balanced faith because one is missing "the grounding, earthiness, and necessary pain that only real involvement within a concrete-parish-type family can give you." I had come to learn over the past two and a half years that mine was, like all parishes, "a hand of cards that are randomly dealt to us, and precisely to the extent that it is truly inclusive, will include persons of every temperament, ideology, virtue, and fault." Maybe I already belonged here, unbaptized and full of doubts as I was. All I knew was that I couldn't leave. Paul felt the same way, and while we agonized over the many horrors of sexual abuse, cover-ups, discrimination, and weaponization of the Scripture, the people in the pews were the reason we couldn't leave. We couldn't hand the church over to the ones we were angry at.

Referring to the German theologian Frederick Schleiermacher, Rolheiser asserts that "the search for God is not a private search for what is highest for oneself or even what is ultimate for oneself. Spirituality is about a communal search for the face of God—and one searches communally only within a historical community." He further claims, "separate from historical religion, namely, the churches with all their faults, the individual in quest of God, however sincere that search, lives the unconfronted life. Without church, we have more private fantasy than real life. . . . Real conversion demands that eventually its recipient be involved in both the muck and the grace of actual church life." It was exactly the muck and grace, I realized, that I wanted to be initiated into. The muck and grace was where I wanted to belong, return to, and be sent forth from.

Easter passed and I met with Fr. P for the first time, anticipating finishing my final two inquiry sessions. Instead, he said we should plan for my catechumen ceremony. "Becoming a catechumen is called your Rite of Acceptance, and it's your official welcoming into the church," he explained. A catechumen is one who is "under instruction" by the church while progressing toward their sacraments of initiation. The ceremony is held during Mass. The RCIA study guide notes that "the prerequisite for making this first step is that the beginnings of the spiritual life . . . have taken root in the candidate." There must be evidence of a "first faith."

Fr. P chuckled. "I think you've done that first part."

"I'm glad it all counted for something," I replied. "I wouldn't mind finishing inquiry. I would just need it to . . . go differently."

"There's no official need to hold six sessions. That's just a number that got picked and so it's taken as a rule after a while." He took out his phone. "There are a few things that need to lead up to the ceremony, but let's get a date on the calendar. We can work backward from there."

We chose Sunday, June 19, two days after my thirty-fifth birthday. After so much waiting, things were beginning to move quickly. Fr. P gave me a copy of the *United States Catholic Catechism for Adults*. He warned me that it was not a page-turner, but it would be helpful in answering a lot of technical and historical questions. "We'll meet every few weeks to prepare," he said. "And after, as you prepare for baptism."

Before I could share the news with Sr. V, I received an email from her. The subject line was "Sad News" and her message explained that she was being transferred, immediately, to her order's main house on the East Coast. We could not continue spiritual direction long distance. She would be buried in her new role as Associate Provincial of her order, an enormous administrative undertaking. She would not be there for my catechumen ceremony or my baptism. My excitement was swiftly pricked by sorrow and deflated. I could feel myself tensing, bracing. I was steeled, ready to white knuckle my way, blindly and alone as I had always done. I wasn't alone, but I had come to see Sr. V as a mentor, someone to lend me experience and insight, to serve as a guide. Our sessions always left me thoughtful, eager to pray, and deeply satisfied, perhaps because my initiation hungers were being fed. I wished her well in this new phase of life and work and tried not to push away the grief that accompanied her move.

In truth, no one can receive their sacraments alone. Sacraments are offered and given, they are witnessed and sponsored. Before my catechumen ceremony, Fr. P asked me to choose a sponsor, someone not unlike a godparent, to serve as a spiritual companion and resource. My husband was the one I already turned to with my hesitations, doubts, and questions, or for help when my prayer life felt arid. He buoyed me with passages from Scripture and theology. In the spirit of *The Screwtape Letters*, we gave absurd names to the dark voices that sought to separate us from God, and he helped me discern my Screwtape voice from God's voice, and from the dozen other competing voices of envy, rivalry, scarcity, and fear. He was already, had been all this time, my sponsor. I worried about putting him in the role of my mentor and not my partner, but he assured me, when he accepted the role, that we were very much on the road together. He often laid bare before me his spiritual struggles, uncertainties, and frustrations, and I was glad to offer what solace or Scripture I thought might help. Noticing where God was present for Paul helped hone my own senses and attunement.

When we first started attending Mass, I needed his presence to anchor me and cue all my motions. After almost a year, I finally went alone for the first time on a Sunday evening because I had slept off a cold during that morning's Mass, and realized how much he grounded my experience of the liturgy, how much he was part of what settled me. That evening on my own, back at the university church where we had first encountered the liturgy as a family, I made it all the way to the Prayer of the Faithful with accuracy and flawless timing. But after the deacon read the first petition, rather than offering the correct response, "Lord, hear our prayer," I confidently and rather loudly boomed, "Lord, have mercy!" My chest heaved until the closing hymn with suppressed laughter at my hapless worship, at the anticipation of Paul's laughter when I returned and told him what I said, at the idea that I needed anything but myself in this space.

Suddenly, I didn't mind that I would ask for and receive acceptance into a new role in the church during Mass and in front of everyone. Turns out, Sr. M had been right all along: when I was ready, the things that bothered me would no longer bother me. My period of inquiry, marked far more by resistance than instruction, was over. The day I became a catechumen would not be my first day of belonging to the church. In my public declaration of wanting to belong, I would know that I already did.

REDEMPTION STORY

The scene is from Luke 2:15. Jesus has been born, and the three Magi
have followed a star and its divine message to Bethlehem, where
they gather with shepherds to behold the infant for themselves. I
am instructed to imagine the setting in detail—the smell of the
animals and afterbirth, the strangers on pilgrimage, the texture
of the manger's edges, the squall of the new Messiah. The scene
is so familiar and worn that even I, an unreligious child from an
immigrant community, know it well. In trying to see the birth anew,
I must detach it from the legion of lawn decorations and animated
Christmas specials that saturate my consciousness every winter. I
must begin to appreciate the gravity, danger, and awe of the moment.
Then, I am to place myself *there*.

As I learn a new form of prayer called composition of place, my
imagination rebels. Also called imaginative prayer, the practice of
placing oneself in a Gospel scene comes from St. Ignatius of Loyola,
whose compilation of prayers, meditations, and reflections titled
The Spiritual Exercises includes guidance on how to contemplate the
Gospels through our imagination. This meditative form of prayer
uses our full set of senses to cultivate intimacy and helps us hear
God speaking to us through our imagination. Then we attend to the
feelings stirred up by the scene. A guide to the Spiritual Exercises
explains that this kind of prayer "is not simply remembering [the
Gospel story] or going back in time. Through the act of contemplation, the Holy Spirit makes present a mystery of Jesus' life in a way
that is meaningful for you now."

In my first attempts, I find composition of place uncomfortable and impossible. The members of the faith-sharing group I've joined have all been practicing this prayer too. In our sharing circle, one woman describes herself at Mary's side, like a midwife, cleaning and swaddling the infant Jesus, almost too afraid to tend his fragile body. A man in our group sees himself as a shepherd, too worried about his flock to fully take in the Savior before him. Their encounters are powerful, and they are visibly moved by their proximity to Jesus, by the revelation of their anxieties and desires, and the gift of their own imagination.

I am nowhere with this kind of prayer. To visualize myself accompanying Jesus requires defiance of all the boundaries of story that I know. Besides, where does a forty-something Chinese American mother from the twenty-first century belong in the Nativity scene? How would I even justify my bewildering presence among the Holy Family? Every time I try, I can conjure the scene vividly, but the picture cuts to static when I try to take my place in it. The same thing happens when I try to imagine I am at the banks of the Jordan River for Jesus's baptism, or at Golgotha for his crucifixion. I feel that in order to occupy any Gospel scene, I have to imagine myself looking like someone who is not Chinese, and I give up.

Until I remember that I imagined myself inside stories for most of my childhood. I put myself into nearly every television show and movie I'd ever watched. I loved episodic television the best, any series with a new weekly crime or mystery I could easily slot myself into—a patient on *ER*, a witness on *NYPD Blue*. I could even fashion myself into an almost-historical migrant on *Dr. Quinn, Medicine Woman*. I rewrote the script as it played out, making room for myself and inventing any reason for being in the story. If I couldn't find a way to play more or less myself, I would just take the place of an existing character, even if they were white, take up their life for a while, and feel everything for them during my hour of borrowed intimacies.

My childhood home was silent, a place where equanimity was prized above all. Emotions, especially unpleasant ones but even exuberant ones, distressed or overwhelmed my parents. Strong feelings were like a virus against which they shielded themselves. The place for feeling and expression was on television, which I watched almost constantly. I didn't escape into books until closer to high school, learning to accompany characters rather than impose myself on them. But television was my early and easy portal into worlds that flared with drama and then resolved neatly in under an hour. I watched, treasure hunting for moments of expression and connection, but missing the larger narrative and the delights of suspense, plot twists, irony, resolution. I felt by approximation and mimesis. Feelings that were not mine were better than nothing, even if only tried on and returned.

Entering the prayer of composition of place, I collide with my old disappearing and with the belief that because feelings threaten equilibrium, my dealings with them must remain scripted and vicarious, and that I am never the protagonist. Like so much of my new faith life, imaginative prayer is a healing and a betrayal, a grief and a hope for my own imagination.

〜

My mom has three stories. The first is about leaving China with her mother when she was twelve years old. The harrowing details of their escape, under cover of darkness and financed by my grandmother's jewelry, engrossed me as a child. The second is about marrying my dad two weeks after they met, and only because of a last-minute twist that brought my dad, and not my dad's cousin, to their blind date. The third is about my grandmother walking out during dinner, but this one is not a story so much as a pulse of memory, gushing forth anytime my mom eased the pressure on the wound. My grandmother was making dinner, my mom somewhere around age ten. A famine was beginning to choke their country, forcing my grandmother to stretch one cup of rice into many bowls of thin porridge. Sometimes there were scraps of wild onion and garlic from the parched yard. But there had always been fermented fish called haam ngui, literally salty fish, deeply pungent, almost rotting. A pinch on the end of your chopsticks was enough to season a whole bowl of rice. Except there was no haam ngui one night, and so my mom cried. My grandmother said nothing as she put on her shoes and took up her umbrella, heading out the door because her ungrateful child dared to cry for food they did not have. She would rather leave than be with such a child. My mom, frantic and weeping, begged her mother to stay, promising never to complain about anything again. Her mother returned silently, and they all ate their unseasoned meal together. It was a strange scrap to tell as frequently as my mom did. Usually, she offered it unprompted, the memory jarred from the dark perhaps by my own food refusals or a whiny kid in a commercial.

My mom never stopped craving haam ngui, though I wonder if its flavor was marred by abandonment. She served it at every meal, which was incomplete until we passed around the briny knob, no bigger than an eraser, that had been plumped back to life in the steaming rice pot, then topped with shaved ginger and oil. We scraped at it carefully, taking only one flaky morsel at a time even though we had enough in the pantry for months of dinners. Our palates were set to haam ngui's savory punch, its stinky blossom transforming our hunger to fullness.

From my mom's stories, I took in what I could and conjured the rest. I invented all kinds of timelines, faces, and dialogue, building the world that came with my mom fleeing her home, her new marriage, her lesson that crying for food would result in terror. If I jumped in to ask for a new detail—*What kind of jewelry did Ah Hoo sell to pay the boatman? Did you get any haam ngui the next day?*—she waved me off, shook her head, and resumed on the very word I had disrupted. Sometimes she talked right through my questions, like a car whose brakes had cut out. I thought my grandmother was wicked for pretending to leave her daughter over such a small offense. But my mom revered her, and I could never have spoken badly of my grandmother. So the story I came to believe was that good mothers made such threats to keep their daughters from crying over what they could not have.

Any story my mom told, even just the itinerary of a recent trip, needed to come out all at once, almost desperately. In the telling, my mom disappeared. She became a net of words, strangled by her own recounting, and unable to talk about other things until the story was over. Sometimes she repeated it, sometimes more than once, always with the same words, order, inflection, and pacing. Around other people, her automated monologue could cause eyes to glaze over, but she never noticed while locked in the contours of a story's groove. My mom often grew breathless in the telling, trying to keep up with a story running ahead of her, which she could see unfolding because she was not recalling the story but living it again, every time. She did not look at me or notice whether I was listening. I stopped asking questions. Afterward, I would collapse into bed because my mom's stories often came after her long day at the restaurant. I slept under these weightless ghosts and escaped into television the next day to disrupt the loop in which her stories endlessly wound me.

—

There are many names for the place my mom is from. She uses Ai Lok for the whole country of China, which translates as "big six" and also sounds like "big green," but may ultimately be a mistranslation of the two characters that compose the word for *mainland*. I never heard her use the Cantonese Jung Gok for China, which translates as "middle country" or "middle kingdom." My mom said, "Heng Ha," when talking about the area her family was from, but it was more used to refer to the countryside or rural villages. Hoi Ping (Kaiping on the maps) is the name for the area of Guangdong Province where my mom's family had lived, at the very southern tip of the country, about 150 miles west of Hong Kong and 1,500 miles south of Beijing. But the name of our dialect of Cantonese, Hoi San, came from the neighboring region's name (Taishan on the maps). Li Hong Lei was a name for my mom's town, but I'd only heard her use it a handful of times. American place names were just as varied and unofficial. My mom's new country was called Mei Gok, which meant "beautiful country." California was Gam Saan, for "gold mountain." Los Angeles was Loo Saang, but that just sounded like an approximation of the English. Two other major Chinese cities in California were Ai Fau (big port) for San Francisco, and Ngi Fau (second port) for Sacramento. All the rest we said in English.

The summer I graduated from high school, my mom's older sister by eighteen years, Auntie May, called to tell us she was taking us to China, the place that held my mom's culture and language, her food, her identity, the whole of her mystery to me. I was going to see it.

I knew only a few details. I would meet my mom's half-brother, Moon, who had not fled to Hong Kong while their country was collapsing from famine. I wondered how he had survived and raised his own family. In a story my mom told me maybe twice, a boy and a mistress arrived with my grandfather upon his return from working abroad in the Philippines, shortly after my mom had been born. My grandmother had fainted at the sight of them, right on the dock where she had come to welcome her husband home. She chased the other woman away with a broom—did she find a broom somewhere near the water's edge, or did this happen later at home?—then took the boy in as her own. He was kind to her youngest daughter. We would also meet my grandmother's brother and sister-in-law, and their children, who had all remained in the family's village.

I fretted over my Cantonese, which was shaky at best. I could follow elders' conversations, but my thoughts brambled on my tongue. Whenever I was expected to offer greetings or answer questions about school, I always froze and resorted to nodding and smiling. My mom made apologies for me. "Saek heng, msaek gong," she would cluck, meaning, "She understands but can't speak." My glacial and choppy Cantonese launched me back to being four years old and spending every day in our family's restaurant. If I imagined myself in the restaurant, suddenly the words came smoothly and confidently, albeit in a child's limited vocabulary. But outside of that building, my fluency evaporated. Words I knew well lost their meaning or hid from me.

My cousin was organizing the trip. He was born only a year after my mom, in his father's neighboring village, where he lived until Auntie May brought him to Hong Kong at age five. I envied how easily he spoke with his mom and mine. He called my mom by her first name, without the honorific of Auntie, blurring the usually rigid generational divides of authority and deference. And now he was planning this trip for seven of us—himself and his wife, two of their daughters, me, my mom, and Auntie May. My dad didn't fly, a combination of phobia, nausea, and generally faring poorly outside his tight comfort zone. My mom froze spareribs in black bean sauce, soups, and fried rice for him, and gave him permission to supplement with whatever processed or fast food he wanted. His favorites were frozen pot pies, canned chili, and a Filet-O-Fish from McDonald's. My mom and I packed for two weeks of humid weather. One entire suitcase was dedicated to gifts—socks, shirts, lotions, perfumes, pairs of glasses, pairs of sandals, candy, cookies, red envelopes filled with cash, all of which we hoped would make it through customs without any trouble.

After a fifteen-hour flight, we arrived in the Hong Kong peninsula city of Kowloon. The plan was to spend four days here, in a plush hotel with all Western amenities. We quickly leaned into being tourists—getting massages, ordering dessert after every meal, soaking in our jetted tubs. At least, the younger people did all that. My mom and Auntie May spent much of each day hunting through markets for pure gold and jade. They bought whole branches of lychee from street vendors, littering the sidewalks with red rinds and black seeds while they browsed and bargained for hours on end. The jewelry here, they whispered, was high quality, genuine, not mixed with cheap metals or green dye. We devoured noodle soups, poached chicken with ginger scallion sauce, and endless varieties of dumplings and dim sum. We sweated through our clothes minutes after stepping outside and ached for ice-cold sodas in a city where drinks were all served at room temperature. Even in our air-conditioned hotel, the humidity was so high that my towel never dried out between showers.

The city stretched upward, and there seemed hardly an inch of sky between all the towering high-rises. Yet somehow we were still punched with sunlight everywhere we walked. We returned again and again to Nathan Road, a congested shopping and dining thoroughfare in Kowloon. Neon signs buzzed and flickered with offers of everything you could ever want to taste or own. The street churned with British-style double-decker buses. English may have been taught in schools, but we needed Cantonese to navigate every store and restaurant. Hong Kong Cantonese is technically the same language as the one spoken throughout my family's Guangdong Province, with a higher, more nasal pitch and softer consonants. Compared to our Hoi San dialect, though, Hong Kong Cantonese's pronunciation and accent sometimes makes it sound like a completely different language. In my ears, Hong Kong Cantonese is the language of Tuesday afternoons with my mom's oldest friend, Auntie Mabel, drinking tea and shelling pistachios, her raspy laughter flickering into the late evening. Until I came to Hong Kong, the language seemed to belong entirely to these women alone. All languages I knew by what relationship they signaled: Hoi San Cantonese among our family, Guangzhou Cantonese with the shopkeepers in Chinatown, a patois of Hoi San Cantonese, English, and Taiwanese Mandarin just with my Auntie Betty.

My mom ushered us around Kowloon anxiously, reading signs and menus, placing orders, asking shopkeepers for recommendations. But she was flustered and hard on herself. People demanded she speak up and say that again, and still they had trouble understanding her. I had always watched my mom struggle with fluency in English, and now she was doing the same in a language so close to her mother tongue. She translated as best she could for us but couldn't always decipher a phrase or sentence's full meaning. Beneath the skin of every word was a body of metaphor, pun, and Chinese cultural and historical references that she could not decode or convey. When she needed a hair dryer or more soap from our English-speaking hotel, I called down for it. I could no longer help her navigate the outside world, but I could still take on whatever tasks required English.

My mom once told me that during her years in Hong Kong, between the ages of twelve and nineteen, girls at her school mocked her Guangdong accent. She said they had been very cruel and looked down on her as a peasant. That is all she's ever told me of Hong Kong. My cousin asked to see where my mom and grandmother had lived in Kowloon, but my mom couldn't remember. Not once did she reminisce about her life here. She never recognized a street or shop or park. She never let on if something we ate or experienced rang familiar. Hong Kong had been my mom's in-between place, where she and her mother had been safe from the terrors of Mao's Great Leap Forward, but still separated from her other siblings in America, still haunted by the ghost of her recently deceased father. They finally came to California in the massive wave of immigration that followed President Johnson's signing of the 1965 Immigration and Nationality Act. After seven years as a foreigner, my mom began once again as a stranger in a new country.

Our group headed out to catch an early morning ferry to Macau. I had been looking forward to this part of our trip since we'd arrived. We had stayed in the same square mile of Hong Kong for four days, never venturing much farther than the city center or the main shopping streets. I'd wanted to see some sights, but my mom found it too complicated to figure out tourist activities. My mom does not see herself as a city person. She calls herself a villager, a country girl with simple tastes. And she moved through Kowloon the same way she did at home: quickly, eyes down, bottom lip tense and curved in against her teeth. Her eyes darted at every movement around us. In China, I imagined, we would not be welcomed as tourists but as family.

As I packed my pressed and perfumed clothes, still freshly wrapped in tissue paper from the hotel's laundry service, I asked my mom, "How long has it been since you've seen your brother?"

"Half brother," she corrected.

She counted and neatly folded the yuan we had just exchanged, stowing some of it in hidden pockets of her shirt lining. She checked and rechecked our passports and travel visas, her suitcase of gifts, her outfit for the next day. Then she paused and counted on her fingers. "Twenty—wait. *Thirty*-nine years," she said.

—

My mom loves American soap operas. Before I was old enough to go to school, I watched the entire ABC daytime lineup every day from under the prep tables in our family's restaurant, while my mom and aunt sliced vegetables, carved meats, and wrapped dumplings. *Loving* began at 11:30 a.m., the shortest and least liked, followed by *All My Children, One Life to Live*, and my mom's absolute favorite, *General Hospital*. The simple and formulaic dialogue coupled with helpfully exaggerated facial expressions and gestures must have been the perfect way for my mom to enjoy English, and a mild distraction from repetitive labor.

As I grew older, it dawned on me that the point of the soap opera was never to end. The characters cycled through the same conflicts year after year, so that it hardly mattered who was doing the weeping, manipulating, or murder plotting. "I don't know why I like these," my mom said when I pointed this out to her with peak middle schooler snobbery. "I just can't stop watching," she admitted. Even today during visits with her grandchildren, my mom will steal forty-five minutes to stream *General Hospital* on her phone and keep up with her characters. She especially loves the high drama of a kidnapping and ransom or a courtroom battle. But the stories don't stay with her. If asked, she can't really explain what's happening to whom or keep track of past events. She barely registers when one actor replaces another or suddenly morphs into their character's evil twin. Yet she can't miss a moment of their turmoil or strife.

"How do we derive pleasure from emotions that are painful?" Aristotle asks. Why does my mom, with all the real drama of her early life, indulge in these fantasies and manufactured emotions? I would have assumed she'd find soap operas too diluted or that she would seek out something calmer to escape into. Aristotle answers his own question when he continues, "We experience pity when we contemplate the misfortune that has befallen . . . and we experience fear when we contemplate the misfortune that awaits. . . . The experience of pity and fear through the tragedy affects the proper purgation(s) of these emotions." Soap opera is all misfortune and so trades constantly in pity and fear. Arousing both with perpetual drama should let my mom purge herself daily. And yet, what happens when the tragedy never climaxes and resolves? What happens when the pity and fear have no arc to follow and no end, only new characters to take on new horrors and inflict new pain? I wonder if my mom is doing something other than properly arousing and purging these difficult feelings. I wonder if it has something to do with her own stories and storytelling, how the events of her past are inchoate churnings pressing to be released?

Stories, writes Jonathan Gottschall in *The Storytelling Animal*, are organized around problems. "The storytelling mind," Gottschall notes, "is a crucial evolutionary adaptation. It allows us to experience our lives as coherent, orderly, and meaningful. It is what makes life more than a blooming, buzzing confusion." He goes on, "The storytelling mind is allergic to uncertainty, randomness, and coincidence. It is addicted to meaning. If the storytelling mind cannot find meaningful patterns in the world, it will try to impose them. In short, the storytelling mind is a factory that churns out true stories when it can but will manufacture lies when it can't. Our hunger for meaningful patterns translates into a hunger for story."

I think about my mom's soaps and her mechanical, dissociative storytelling, how she gets caught in a soap's sordid webs or her singular moment of panic and near abandonment. They all play continuously and without commentary, all strings of events missing meaningful patterns or any drive toward development or change. The trauma expert Bessel van der Kolk posits that trauma is the loss of our ability to tell the story, because the story gets stuck inside us, forcing us to relive instead of relate the events, inhibiting the integration of the past with the present, and imprisoning the traumatized. As a child, I learned to sit very still, absorbing my mom's flood of story. I made it my task to regulate her, to hold steady through memory's storm, just as I did when she grew agitated at the store clerk who couldn't understand her, at the receipt she could not decipher, at the furious merging of three Los Angeles freeways. Her storytelling mind seemed disrupted by the traumas of famine, separation, immigration, cultural assimilation, and language loss. And she seemed to crave shows with similarly disordered narratives, losing herself in them for three and a half hours a day so that she wouldn't have to lose herself in her own memories. Or her boredom. Hers didn't seem like a hunger for story but for a mirror to her own tangled and knotted experiences.

My mom doesn't like movies or TV series. Only soaps, with all their brooding and scheming and sleek clothes. Any time she tried to sit through something I had rented from Blockbuster, she would quickly grow restless and go to fuss around the kitchen. She would return for a few minutes before her leg started to jiggle and then she would be off to look for something she needed upstairs. In the scant minute of each return, teetering on the edge of the couch and poised to spring up again, she would ask hopefully, plaintively, "It's over?"

⁓

I never thought to ask why neither my grandmother nor my two uncles had come with us to Hong Kong and China. I didn't wonder at the time why this trip wasn't a major family event. My grandmother was in her eighties and my uncles were in their sixties that year. Maybe they were less able to travel than I realized. Or maybe returning to the country they left awash in chaos and starvation was not what any of them wanted.

In 1947, the year my mom was born, China was tipping into crisis. When my mom was two years old, the Communist Party declared itself the new head of China. Within a month of taking power, and with the help of Soviet planes, fuel, and supplies, Mao invaded the western province of Xinjiang, also known as the Uyghur Autonomous Region. Imitating Stalin at every turn, Mao massacred an estimated three million landowners in a purge of the landlord class, then redistributed the land to the people. Four years later, in 1953, many poor farmers could, for the first time, grow enough food to pay duties to the government and feed themselves from land they now owned. But that same year Stalin died, and once he was publicly denounced by Khrushchev in 1956, Mao abruptly ended all programs that had been modeled on Stalinism. He seized all the redistributed land and pooled families into enormous collectives, sometimes by the thousands. Without landlords to scapegoat anymore, the Communist Party came under scrutiny and criticism. In a scheme to entrap his critics, Mao used his Hundred Flowers Campaign, which initially invited all to publicly voice their opinions about the party, under the ancient ideal, "Let a hundred flowers bloom, and a hundred schools of thought contend." Letters poured in and overwhelmingly demanded more freedom, democratic governance, and restrictions on party power. Angered by the outcries, Mao turned on those who spoke out, sending critics to labor or reeducation camps, or executing them.

With fear nationally weaponized, the utter madness of the Great Leap Forward began in 1958, when my mom was eleven years old. That year, her father also died while traveling abroad, his body never to be claimed or brought home. In the meantime, Mao mobilized the masses into campaigns that could only be described as absurd, and only for the purposes of distracting, subduing, and doling out fruitless ambition and false idols to millions of peasants. Farmers were diverted from their fields to fulfill half-baked civil projects in mining and steel production in a bid to out-industrialize the West. Threats and enemies were created everywhere—in the rich, the educated, the foreigners, the individualists, and even the lowly sparrow in the Four Pests Campaign. Identified as a crop pest, sparrows were hunted nearly to extinction, which only made way for an explosion of locusts and the destruction of millions of tons of crops.

In the Western imagination, Mao isn't always first in mind when we think of genocide and torture, systemic brutality, suppression, and egomania. But the Great Chinese Famine of 1958–61, spurred in part by the sparrow killings, was the largest famine in human history, killing between 36 and 45 million.

What I know of my mom and grandmother's escape in 1959 takes up less than a page. My grandmother sold most of her jewelry to pay for boat passage out of Guangdong. When she and my mom arrived at the boat, a man demanded more, and my grandmother tore off all the pieces she was wearing and handed them over. Secretly, though, she had sewn the most valuable pieces into her clothing. Though I have not been able to confirm this with any sources, my mom remembers having to say that she was eleven rather than twelve. No one is sure whether it was China or Hong Kong or rogue agents that required children to be under twelve to leave. But because of this change, my mom's immigration and identification documents list her birth year as 1948 instead of 1947. Numerous times she has bemoaned having to work an extra year before being able to retire.

The rest of the story I can only guess or glean from other sources, filling in the gaps mostly with books. I don't know what my mom survived during that year before her escape, while farms were destroyed by party leaders ordering crops to be grown on land unsuitable for them, and while farmers were brutalized for not inflating crop output numbers. I can only assume that she endured starvation, but for how long? An entire year? More? I don't know how quickly Mao's policies reached her remote village, while all around, autonomy was outlawed, private property abolished, and communal living separated men, women, and children, destroying both nuclear and extended families. I devoured history books that exposed how China's population was used toward impossible, preposterous, and catastrophic ends, its people unmoored from any sense of stability or family so they would follow their leader into ruin and starvation. From historical maps, I learned that my mom's province, Guangdong, is not listed as one of the "hardest hit" provinces. The highest number of famine casualties come from regions north and east of hers, Henan in particular, where one in eight citizens starved to death. I read that only one year after her escape, Hong Kong severely restricted movement across its historically open border with China. All I know for certain is that because of Mao's policies, my mom inhabits a moment of longing for salty fish, of aching, of her mother leaving because she dared to hunger.

My mom's story collides with my history books in an event larger than any other of its kind. Though touched by Mao's madness, by the disasters he created and others enabled, and which the world chose to believe were caused simply by drought, my mom is not a history. What lives on in her brittle bones, her hoarding tendencies, her scarcity mindset, and her many anxieties, is not a ghost or haunting or even past. I have known her to be happy at times, even to laugh deeply. But the space she occupies is never entirely present. Part of her is always missing, too busy with vigilance or remembering. Her entire country's memory gaps are vast. Historians have risked their lives to reveal the true horrors of Mao's initiatives that were covered up by the party, the rampant cannibalism in particular. Officials hunted down anyone who dared ask for help or reveal the truth. The historian Yang Jisheng laments, "Our history is all fabricated. It's been covered up. If a country can't face its own history, then it has no future."

And what future is there for a person who cannot face their history? Bessel van der Kolk explains that we "shut down the brain areas that transmit the visceral feelings and emotions that accompany and define terror" to defend against pain. "Yet," he continues, "in everyday life, those same brain areas are responsible for registering the entire range of emotions and sensations that form the foundation of self-awareness, our sense of who we are. . . . In an effort to shut off terrifying sensations, they also deadened their capacity to feel fully alive."

When I boarded the ferry heading for my mom's birthplace, I didn't yet know all she had left. I hadn't yet learned about how her country had deceived and used and abandoned its people, how her home had become a nightmare. I tried to picture my mom at my age, eighteen: five feet tall, high cheekbones, the same narrow nose as my grandmother, waiting in a loud, crashing city by the water to see her sister and brothers again. I pictured her at twelve: bowl haircut, thin and frail, teeth loose from malnutrition. But the place of every picture is where her storytelling mind was fractured.

Our ferry moved steadily enough for me not to get seasick, unlike my poor aunt. There were two levels, both with wraparound decks and sheltered seating, along with a restaurant where we ordered wide rice noodles in oxtail soup, fragrant with Chinese five spice. Other passengers guarded their bags and brightly wrapped boxes, clutched bouquets and tins of cookies to present to whomever they would be meeting. I drew my headphones over my ears after an hour. I had forgotten to pack any music, so the one CD I had was the one left in my Discman before we had left LA—Shakira's recently released *Dónde Están los Ladrones?* It was a fitting album for the trip. My senior Spanish teacher had given us extra credit for translating the album as poetically as possible, and the songs flooded me with premature nostalgia for high school, which had ended just a month before. After four years of study and a trip to Mexico, I could think in Spanish while in conversation, which I could never do in Cantonese. While cramming for my AP exam, I even had an entire dream in Spanish. It had become my language of escape, a reprieve from the one that separated me from my mom and the other I could barely grasp anymore.

When the city came into view, my mom said her brother would meet us at the station. He had arranged for a pair of trucks to take us and our luggage to the village.

"I call him *m-ai-kyue?*" I asked, stashing away my music. My mom nodded. Such a succinct way to say "fifth eldest uncle on the mother's side."

I knew only a handful of details about my Uncle Moon. He had been rather lazy and shiftless, skipping school, stealing fruit from neighbors to sell in town for cigarette money, running away, secretly eloping. But he had also walked my mom to school every morning and chased away girls who bullied her.

"How do you say?" My mom searched for a word. "He used to be such a *brat*."

Over the years, through an exchange of letters with Uncle Moon's wife, my mom learned that he had become a cook at a school for boys, the very one he himself had been sent to as a teenager. My uncle could not read or write, but he wanted his wife to send us a letter saying that he had fixed up the house, part of which had been destroyed in a fire years ago. I wondered what the space between Uncle Moon and my mom would hold. In Sacramento, my mom was always instantly at ease among her three siblings. My uncles Yee Man and Yee Don were quiet and steady men, with soft voices and slow gestures. Uncle Yee Man could sit all evening on an old folding chair in his garage just gazing at the still street, the smoke from his Kings cigarettes wafting into the honeysuckle.

The ferry lurched hard as we entered the harbor. We lost our grip on our packages and watched them slide into the far wall. The people next to us flew out of their seats and hit the hard wooden floor on their hands and knees. We all collected ourselves and our belongings and waited for the platform to ease down like a drawbridge connecting us to China. It was noon, achingly hot, and only slightly less humid than Kowloon. The station looked like any bus or train station in America: cement floors, vending machines, posters and schedules peeling off the walls, ticket agents behind glass partitions. We presented our passports and visas to the agents, each backed by a guard in an olive uniform, a machine gun strapped across his chest. As we walked through the station door and toward the parking lot, my mother fixed her gaze beyond the high gate and pointed confidently at a man with dark, leathery skin, hands in pockets, leaning against the seat of a motorcycle.

"That's him?" I asked.

I tried to keep my eyes on the man as heads bobbed in front of me and sharp shoulders flung me off balance. He looked tall and gaunt, his thin clothes hanging loosely on him. His face seemed tired, his mouth a little turned down. He stood, not smiling, not quite frowning, watching people pass through the gate.

"Yes, there," my mom said. "On the bike."

Other passengers edged past us, greeting their parties with shouts. But we went slowly, my mom looking at her feet as she walked. My aunt and cousins struggled to wheel their suitcases through the crowd. As we pushed through the turnstile and out of the station, Uncle Moon stood up straight and drew his hands out of his pockets. He saw us. My mom emerged before her brother and set her bag down between them. They held each other's eyes for a moment, then my mom nodded at him and put out her hand. Uncle Moon took her right hand in his, then put his left hand over them both. He nodded to her, and then they let go.

"Ah-Len," her brother said.

"Ah-Moon," my mother replied.

My mom stepped aside, and Auntie May walked up, took Uncle Moon's hand in hers the same way my mom had, and he nodded in return.

"Ah-Nay."

"Ah-Moon."

Uncle Moon met my cousin, his wife, and their daughters.

"Ah-Moon," my mother called, pointing at me. "This is my daughter, Fui Gehn. She is going to college."

I stood there dumbly with my bag bearing down on my shoulder. Uncle Moon nodded at me, looking at my face with a sure, quiet recognition, as if he had seen me every day of my life. Taking my cue from my mother and aunt, I said softly, "M-ai-kyue."

He nodded at me, we took each other's hands, and he said my name in return. Then he said something else. It took me a moment to hear, to translate. I had never heard the family dialect outside of our home. "Ah-Gehn, ni ho goh ah!" (You are very tall), he exclaimed.

There were two trucks waiting for us. The drivers stepped on their cigarettes and loaded our bags into the cabs, stuffing them under a rack of built-in wire cages stuck with white feathers. I sat by the window and my mom squeezed in next to me, our knees touching the front seats in the cramped cabin. My aunt, exhausted and seasick, pressed in on the other side of my mom and laid her forehead against her window, while my cousins folded themselves into the second truck. We pulled away from the station, following Uncle Moon on his motorcycle away from the town and toward the village. His white shirt billowed out behind him as he weaved through traffic. I was quiet for a while, and then I couldn't hold it in any longer.

"A handshake?" I asked my mom. "Just a handshake?"

I hadn't expected shrieks or spinning hugs, but I was surprised there hadn't been more, after thirty-nine years, fifteen hours on a plane, four long days in Hong Kong, and a choppy four-hour ferry ride.

"What?" My mom shrugged, never taking her eyes off the front window. "This is how we say hello."

⁓

The countryside of Guangdong was silent. It was a deep, heavy silence that swallowed us whole. We stopped frequently to let gaunt cows cross from one field to another. I put my head out the window at each stop and listened to the emptiness, to the herds that moved noiselessly across the gravel road, trailed by a man flicking a thin switch near their rumps. We passed shimmering rice paddies and drooping orchards, the fields broken occasionally by gray stone houses. A few yards from the road, I saw three men bent over some freshly sown rows, each in a white shirt and wide bamboo hat. As we passed, they all straightened at the same time, turning to watch our caravan of motorcycle and rusty chicken trucks piled with luggage. As if choreographed, they leaned against their wooden hoes in unison and drew their free hands up to shade their eyes and watch us disappear. Had these fields once sat ruined and razed, this road a collection of corpses only forty years ago, in the living memory of most, my Uncle Moon included?

The village came upon us suddenly, after an hour of driving. First a fence, then a single, slouching outhouse were the only buildings among the farmlands. Then, suddenly, we were surrounded: gray cement houses standing close together, chicken coops, barns, fields of goats, and people everywhere. Children running, elders squatting around mah-jongg boards, men on bicycles, women wrangling animals. People stopped and stared, then encircled us.

My mother gave out every last shirt and pair of socks to the crush of children with dusty, sunburned faces and outstretched hands. I stood as they fingered my jeans and prodded my sneakers, calling me "Ai-Yee" and "Sui-Jen" (Auntie and Miss). I tried to talk to them in faltering Cantonese. Instead of asking their names, I blurted, "Who are you?" As we were turning to leave, how to say "goodbye" suddenly escaped me. So I waved and said, "See you tomorrow."

My mother sighed at the group of children as we turned to leave them. "Hard to live like this when you are young," she murmured.

We grabbed our bags and began walking behind Uncle Moon along a path no wider than a bicycle tire, ducking beneath branches every few steps. The houses on either side were gray and white, square, stone, framed with worn shutters, sometimes with lucky red banners over the doorways. We were all quiet. The house, my mom's house, finally appeared, and out of the front door, a line of women made their way toward us. They lifted our bags onto their own shoulders, giving us quick pats on the arm, nodding and smiling. They had short, jagged haircuts and wore loose cotton pants and shirts. Their bronze faces shone with curiosity. There was a shy teenage girl in a pristine white dress and matching shoes, holding a lacy parasol. She was, I realized, dressed up for *us*.

The women's voices and hands fluttered around us. "Ah-Len! Kwan Yim Len. This is your daughter? She is tall. Do you speak Chinese? Do you understand me?"

I smiled and nodded again and again, shaking hands and saying, "I speak a little" and "thank you."

They led us inside and gestured to empty chairs around a wooden dining table. Mugs of tea appeared before us along with pieces of candy my mom had brought. My uncle, eager to cook us lunch, went outside to pull up vegetables and wash some rice. One auntie carried in an armload of straw and wood. Crouching before the wide iron stove, she smiled and waved me over. I bent down next to her as she reached beneath the stove's belly and drew out a squirming newborn kitten, a dark twist of umbilical stump still jutting from its translucent belly. She handed it to me and brought out three more, all variations of orange tabby, their eyes still closed and their mewling fierce. I cooed over them and said, "Cute," in Cantonese. She laughed and returned them to their warm hideout. I had only ever heard the word used for children and wondered now if maybe it didn't apply to animals.

The house was cozy and narrow, the concrete floors covered with thin rugs, the walls displaying red calendars, embroidered handkerchiefs, Chinese movie star posters, and small family photos taped down at the corners. The previous year, my uncle had installed a water pump in the kitchen, delivering a thin stream into the bucket they used as a sink. My mom once told me a spring flood had forced my grandmother to unhinge the front door for them to float around the house until the waters receded. She told me another time that on one of his rare visits home, my grandfather had carried her, half asleep, upstairs to bed. I didn't know how to ask her about all these things now that we were here. They suddenly seemed less real, less vivid than before.

The kitchen was hot and busy, so my mom and I wandered upstairs where there were four tidy bedrooms, their windows draped in sheer pink fabric. She wasn't giving me a tour so much as taking in the rooms along with me. She didn't remember which bedroom had been hers. I sat down on one of the beds with a thud. There was no mattress, only a quilt and pillows over wooden boards. Peering beneath the bed, my mom exclaimed, "Look!" She laughed and pointed to a porcelain bowl. "You know what that is?"

"Yes." I nodded.

"The bathroom!" she exclaimed anyway.

We moved through the rest of the upstairs and my mom posed for a picture in one of the doorways before we made our way outside. Vegetables grew everywhere, squash tangling up wooden stakes and chicken wire, orderly rows of spinach and garlic and chives. Next to a small pond sat stacks of tubs and scrub boards. I noticed then, for the first time in days, what my mom was wearing: a red T-shirt, flowered capri pants, and brown sandals. It was a stifling afternoon, and her makeup was running a little. Her appearance startled me.

She looked so bright against the village's worn gray. Suddenly, in her Calvin Klein sunglasses, highlighted hair, and leather purse, she looked as American as a Colgate commercial.

Just then, Uncle Moon called to us from a screenless kitchen window. "Ah-Len. Ah-Gehn. Lai-ah. Ne gai gok ho loh." (Linda. Melody. Come in. The chicken is cooked.)

Lunch was all set out when we came inside. Several wooden tables had been pushed together. Neighbors and cousins fanned themselves and waited eagerly. We sat down to dishes of greens, melon soup, steamed chicken, yams, bean sprouts, rice, haam ngui, and persimmon slices, all spread to the tables' edges. Uncle Moon lit three sticks of incense and set them in a cup in the middle of the food. Behind us stood an ancestor worship altar with sketched portraits of my great-grandparents and the names of my great-great-grandparents inked in gold on a red scroll. I watched the elders bless our food with words and gestures I vaguely recognized from the rituals my grandmother used to perform before our holiday meals. Someone loaded a plate and set it on the altar for the ancestors to have the first taste. The food was divine, scorching hot, with flavors at once strong and delicate, familiar and exotic. We ate quietly. We caught my uncle's eye and offered the compliment "Ho mei," which means "good flavor."

Just as quickly as it had come together, the empty plates disappeared into a bucket for washing, the tables were pulled apart, and my mom brought out the last of her gifts for the family—the fattest red envelopes for the eldest relatives, the envelopes with single bills or half dollars for the tiny nieces and nephews and neighbor kids. The aunties asked for more, grasping my mom's hands and pleading with her to think of their hard lives. My mom reached for some extra cash sewn into her clothes and handed out every dollar.

Evening arrived, the neighbors dispersed, and it was time for us to check into our hotel in town. Uncle Moon walked us back down the same path we'd come in on. The same drivers, who must have spent the afternoon nearby, visiting whom and doing what I had no idea, suddenly appeared and gathered us back into the trucks. My mom told Uncle Moon we would see him tomorrow. He waited and watched until we were on our way before heading back to the house. In town, our hotel felt like an alternate universe from the village with no plumbing. I was grateful for the air conditioning and hot showers, the electric kettle, and the complimentary assortment of fragrant teas.

Neither my mom nor her relatives had spoken much all day. I didn't know what I had expected anyone to say at this reunion, which had felt nothing like a homecoming. By the end of high school, I understood that my parents' home was not where I felt most myself or at ease, and that it would not be my home for much longer. I had known that this trip would not be my mom's return home, exactly. And yet, I had come on this trip to find her. I had expected the mystery of her to unravel here. That in her hometown, her first source of language, food, identity, and comfort, where she had learned her name, where her family had been intact, I would see her real self, which I had imagined was obscured by her persistent unease in America. I had thought that in a place where she didn't chafe against everything, including her American daughter, she might shed her weariness. But not even in China, the place from which she drew her expectations and norms, the place for which she grieved and yearned, was she at home. She was just as foreign on the plot of land where she had been born as she was in America. After all this time, we had returned to the site of her life story's disruption, to the page where the words skidded to a blank. We had come all this way, but she was nowhere to be found.

⁓

Over our next three days in Guangdong, our relatives came to town to see us. We never went back to the village. Different family members came each day—Uncle Moon, my mom's maternal uncle and aunt, a young cousin who asked how we could help him get into a U.S. college. We took them to lunch and showed them around the hotel, where they laughed at our mattresses and envied our microwave. Out of nowhere, my mom produced more red envelopes to distribute.

My great-uncle, wiry and agile, took us shopping at a street market, speed walking and telling us to keep up. He led us to a vendor he liked and instructed us to show him what we wanted. I held up a black T-shirt and smiled.

"This is the one you want?" he asked in Cantonese. I nodded.

"Hey!" he barked to the shopkeeper. "My niece wants a shirt like this, but in another color, not this ugly one. What else do you have?"

I tried to protest, but he put his hand up to silence me. "This can't be the only one you have. What a shame! She doesn't like it."

The shopkeeper apologized and started tearing through a box of shirts as high as her waist. My great-uncle winked at me.

"Miss, miss! I guess we have to take this black one. But why should we pay full price for a shirt she doesn't even want?"

He did this again and again for anything my mom or I wanted. I caught on that I only needed to touch an item and he would hoist it up and complain about its size, material, or pattern, and get the price lowered by half. He smirked and strutted through the entire market. For the first time during our trip, I felt at ease, following my stooped but hale elder as he charged up and down stall aisles, croaking about how a pair of sunglasses I had eagerly grabbed was unworthy of even one yuan. My great-uncle knew how things worked here. His voice was commanding. I trusted him completely when he said to buy these shoes and not those, this necklace and not that one, and when he hurried us away from aggressive shopkeepers calling, "Hey, hey, pretty girl, try this on!" I knew this uncle had looked after my grandmother while my grandfather had traveled frequently for work. I imagined he used his guile and confidence to give his widowed sister and her children a voice and a chance at survival.

Because I couldn't form the question in Cantonese, I asked my mom to ask her uncle if these shopkeepers were losing money because of us. He responded, "Ni gong muat gui, ah!" Literally translated as, "What the devil are you saying?," in this context, the phrase was closer to, "The hell they are!" My great-uncle assured us they were all turning plenty of profit because they inflated their prices whenever they saw foreigners coming. He jutted his chin at me and my mom, the foreigners. We bought him a sticky rice dumpling and a bottle of green tea as a thank you, then plodded back to the hotel, exhausted from the haggling and hauling of all our treasures.

Before we left Guangdong, we wandered another street market, just our little American crew. We bought last-minute gifts and trinkets, moving at a frenzied pace to spend our yuan and remember China. One stall, packed to the ceiling with whole, three-foot-long haam ngui, reeked of comfort and decay. My mom and aunt bought two fish each despite my cousin's protests and worry about U.S. customs. These, they said, you could not get in even the best shops in Chinatown. My mom wrapped each one in multiple shopping and laundry bags and nestled their stiff bodies among her clothes.

Our family goodbyes at the hotel were clipped and muted. There were pleas and promises to come again soon, to help them visit us in America, to help their kids go to college, to stay in touch, and come more often. There were handshakes and shoulder pats, a gift of oranges for us, and, unbelievably, more red envelopes my mom kept drawing out of thin air like trick cards. There were moist eyes and no hugs.

Eastern jet streams shortened our return journey by nearly two hours. My mom devoured her semi-American meal of grilled chicken and pasta, then slept restlessly for a good portion of the flight. But not before saying, unbidden, "I couldn't live there anymore." She meant the place we had just departed from, with its lack of facilities and opportunity, the debilitating poverty and uncertainty, and its culture that no longer belonged to her. She also meant that where she *could* live was America.

⁓

When attempting the imaginative prayer called composition of place, my urge is still to disappear into a Gospel character. I want to inhabit the prodigal son who was welcomed home with a fatted calf, the tax collector Zacchaeus called by name down from a tree by Jesus, or Mary Magdalene discovering Jesus's empty tomb. After many attempts, I can manage to place myself in a crowd, blending in, lurking in the background. I keep at it stubbornly until finally, for the first time, I visualize myself in a scene.

I am at the pool of Bethesda, which is surrounded by five porticoes. In John 5:1, Jesus encounters a sick man who has been lying beside this pool for thirty-eight years, unable to get himself into the healing water ahead of "a large number of ill, blind, lame, and crippled." The story does not specify this man's ailment. I begin by imagining the water and the portico columns made of smooth sand-colored stone and mortar. The sun is bright, as if it's noon. I see and smell the bodies all around, the tattered and stained tunics and dresses barely covering their abscessed wounds and sores. The afflicted crouch, poised to leap into the pool at the first sign of the water stirring, which signals its healing power has been activated. The story continues in John 5:6:

> When Jesus saw him lying there and knew that he had been ill for a long time, he said to him, "Do you want to be well?" The sick man answered him, "Sir, I have no one to put me into the pool when the water is stirred up; while I am on my way, someone else gets down there before me." Jesus said to him, "Rise, take up your mat, and walk." Immediately the man became well, took up his mat, and walked.

I strain to imagine myself in my own body, to see out of my own eyes. In the scene, I, too, have been ailing for a long time and am unable to get to the water. I am lying on a filthy mat. My whole being wonders why no one has helped me all this time. Then I see Jesus kneel before the man. I hear him ask, "Do you want to be well?" When he does, he is looking at me, too. Then Jesus looks beyond us two, and I turn to follow his gaze. There is a crowd of ancient and modern people of all races, all lying on mats, all waiting. We all nod our heads and grumble that no one will help us either. When Jesus tells the man to rise and walk, we all hear that the instructions are for us and do the same. This weary crowd leaves behind the expectation of rescue and the rumors of magical water we no longer need and perhaps never did. And we go on our way. My body feels stiff and achy, but I am walking in the pulsing sunlight. As the vividness of the scene eases to a soft blur, I keep my eyes closed and go from wrestling with myself to just watching.

Upon completing the prayer of composition of place, Ignatius advises that we take inventory of our thoughts and feelings, which are ways we can hear God speaking to us. Many Ignatian spirituality guides note that what happens during composition of place is both created and granted, both an act of your imagination and a gift from God. In the scene at Bethesda, I had felt neglected and resentful at receiving no help into the pool, then relieved upon being healed, then ashamed. I regretted the time I'd spent bitterly awaiting relief but never asking for it, all while I could have risen. I had only to admit that I wanted to be well. Lying stuck at the edge of the pool had been, if not entirely a choice, then perhaps a resignation. A hopelessness. But suddenly it occurs to me, not through my own mental prowess but maybe by what I am learning is grace or mercy, that my waiting had not been a failure but rather a sign of hope, even faith, that healing was possible.

With each breath that settles on this new understanding, the shame dissolves a little and relief settles in. My waiting feels redeemed, and so does my ability to inhabit a story. From the Latin *re* for "back" or "return" and *emere* for "purchase," the word *redemption* means we are bought and restored from captivity, without erasing the captivity. Redemption is not forgiveness. It's not a movie protagonist who falls and then earns their way back to a state of grace, acceptance, or honor. Redemption is not something you can perform for yourself, regardless of any great act of will or change or sacrifice. It means that we are, like the Hebrews out of Egypt, emancipated from our prisons, both imposed and self-made.

⁓

The summer after my sophomore year in college, my mom invited me to China again. It had been two years since we visited Kowloon and Guangdong. This time, it would just be the two of us on a ten-day tour she had booked through a Chinatown travel agency. Our group of twenty Californians included several middle-aged couples, two pairs of newlyweds, one couple in their seventies celebrating their anniversary, two best friends, and my mom and me. The trip was a whirlwind of planes and charter buses through Beijing, Xi'an, Suzhou—cities over a thousand miles apart—and so the trip was planned to the minute. We raced through every tourist site, with no time to wander or marvel before being loaded onto the bus for the next destination. We learned to listen for our guide screeching, "Super Vacation!" and herd ourselves away from the crowd and back to the bus on time. Group meals were banquet style and lasted for hours. My mouth watered at grilled shrimp skewers and red bean shaved ice from sidewalk food carts, but those were not on the itinerary. Neither were cheap souvenirs from street vendors. We were kept to the glistening, high-rise department stores with "Duty Free" labels on everything.

Spats broke out among group members over things like the sharp, fungal smell of someone's new medicinal herbs wafting through the bus, or someone at dinner wailing that she couldn't possibly eat any more rice, then being chastised and hissed at while she cried over her next bowl. At the Great Wall, we all kept to an easy portion with modern handrails, but one woman wandered off and climbed a very high and precarious section, which delayed our return to the hotel for nearly an hour. Boarding the bus where we were all sweltering, she reported a mystical experience that included talking with her dead grandmother at the top. But she refused to tell us what her grandmother had said, and people accused her of telling tales to impress. We were all overtired, joints aching from the long rides and stomachs in upheaval from the unfamiliar food.

I found the tour schedule and pace exhausting, the curation confining. My mom, however, loved it. In the pictures, she smiles brightly as she examines boiled silkworm cocoons in a garment factory, poses at the gates of the Forbidden City, peers down at a row of unearthed terra-cotta soldiers. The whole trip, she was attentive, absorbed, ready to go early each morning and following our schedule to the letter. The only thing she didn't like was the American breakfast buffet in every hotel. She longed for something savory, especially rice porridge topped with chicken and greens, instead of watery scrambled eggs and cream pastries.

My mom has toured China four more times since. She enjoys the safety of a knowledgeable guide and the comforts of an air-conditioned bus. A detailed itinerary eliminates all decision-making and worry. She doesn't need to use Cantonese or the basic Mandarin she has picked up from her mah-jongg friends. She lets my dad, who by then had overcome his fear of flying or perhaps his misery at being home alone, ask the guide questions in English. All my mom needs to do is be at the right places on time.

In all these travels, my mom has never gone back to her village, not even when one tour took her to Fuzhou, a southern city about five hundred miles from her brother and uncle. In an agency-branded hat and name badge, my mom returns and returns to China, ushered and fed, exposed to the pleasant and sanitized slices of Chengdu's teahouses and operas, or the unpolluted banks of the Yellow River at Lanzhou. After my first tour, I declined to go again, so my mom went with my dad, her friends, and then with two of my aunts. They raved about the meals, the shopping, the excellent photo ops. They became experts at the selfie, capturing their faces in most of the frame, with a slice of a Buddhist temple or gravity-defying suspension bridge behind them. Maybe this is how my mom can see her country without fracturing into the past. Maybe she is trying to redeem something of her own with these trips marked by the kind of safety and abundance she had never known as a girl.

By the time my mom and I went to China for the first time, I had not heard her stories in a long time. Before middle school, I had begun retreating from them. I had listened because she always looked relieved, if only a little, by the end, shaking her head and quickly leaving the room and me in a fog of her discharged loss and grief.

At the time, I could not articulate the loneliness of listening to her, of being flooded with a chaos I could not bring to order for either of us. Or of her agitation and memories crowding out any room for stories of my day. So, I stopped asking for or sitting through her stories. Without them, there had been little else to say.

On a visit to St. Louis recently, my parents showed us pictures of a friend's daughter's courthouse wedding. When my mom started describing the photos, her words began unspooling without pause or eye contact. The events were new but had only her worn storytelling channels to move along. My mom became a live wire, shedding sparks for me to catch and extinguish. Her details began to disappear us both. I sat nodding as long as I could, perhaps ten minutes of streaming recollections, before I excused myself to get ready for dinner. When I returned, it was time to head out to the restaurant, but my mom raced to continue the story, which had burst its dam inside her. We sat with car keys in hand, unable to leave.

It was then that I hit a limit. For the first time, and not even fully aware of my own motivations, I jumped in. I could not sit there as a receptacle. My husband and daughters, the most real things in my life, were beside me, and I suddenly wanted my mom to talk *to me*, to all of us. When she began detailing the bride and groom's apartment, I interrupted with, "What city do they live in?"

My mom's face knotted with distress as she stopped to think. "Irvine," she replied, almost looking at me now.

She resumed for a minute, and then I broke in with, "Where did they meet?" I asked for more and more details. "What do they do for work?" "Where is he from?" I pressed on. "How far was the venue from your house?"

Her grimace was a swirl of confusion and betrayal. She replied as if under interrogation. "Not far, I don't know, half an hour? I didn't keep track!" I drew my daughters closer to see the pictures. They, naturally, started pointing and asking questions, making little cooing noises at the flowers and the bride. My mom grew quiet, and her answers shriveled to monosyllables. My girls squealed, "That looks pretty, Grandma. How fun!" But my mom looked under attack. She couldn't pick up the thread. There was no one to gather it all as it wound out of her. "I forgot what I was going to say," she sighed. We headed out to dinner. While sipping jasmine tea, my mom lamented how bad her memory was getting and vowed to brew something with ginkgo that night.

I felt terrible for what I had done to her. Part of me wished I had just let her go on and waited it out as usual. I wished I could experience her stories like Paul, who grew weary but stayed patient and attentive, or like strangers who could often be charmed by her animation. But her stories felt like drowning to me. They always had. The way I'd learned to show love and respect was to keep still and be a container shaped like her daughter. But in forcing my questions—my interest, my voice, my presence—into her storytelling, I seemed to injure her and cause her to withdraw.

Our separation has always been the price of her wounded storytelling mind. Whether it glides along its grooves or is forced off track, we are both entirely alone with each other.

My daughters sometimes ask me about the person I was before they were born. When life feels busy, their questions seem scattered and endless. *What was your favorite food? Who was your best friend? Did you ever wish for a sibling?* When they ask for a story, they want it in exquisite detail, and they burst in with many questions. If I listen closely, I can hear them piecing something together as they dig around my past. Often, their questions reveal their own preoccupations. *Were you scared on your first day of school? Were you embarrassed to get glasses? Were you ever jealous of your best friend? What happened when you got caught passing notes in class?* They are trying to create a coherent picture of me and the world to which they belong a little more each day. They ask in order to feel less alone, to see themselves in my life and me in theirs. When I tell them about myself as a kid, they realize so much about childhood goes unchanged from generation to generation, and that much of the past is simply a mystery. When I tell them stories and answer their questions, we are all consoled.

I am getting so much of my mom's stories—so much of *her*—wrong. There is more I want to know, so much that would make this very writing richer, more complete, more accurate. I know the extent of what my writing lacks, misses, and neglects. I know how much I have formed from my own incomplete and mistaken memory. But I haven't found a way to be present and contained amid her storytelling, to remain available but also assert, *I am here too*.

But now I can at least imagine something else. A story is lying on its mat. It has been waiting for sixty-five years to be healed of many afflictions—terror, deprivation, disorder. And it is trapped inside a mother walking out over salty fish, a stuck record that cannot play past a damaged spot. To be made well is to be shown all the rest of the story: the mother returns. She stays. She takes her daughter to Hong Kong and then all the way to America, where they are spared further catastrophe but not crushing grief, where daughters become mothers and learn, in an entirely new language, that redemption means the story is set free. The story can rise. The story can walk. The story has waited long enough.

TWO ADOPTIONS

I watched *Star Trek: The Next Generation* obsessively as a kid. The episode I most often replayed was "Parallels." Near the end of the episode, the crew of the starship *Enterprise* must repair a strange "quantum fissure," an anomalous area where space and time have been disrupted, and the barriers between alternate realities have broken down. In a climactic scene, space is bombarded with thousands of *Enterprise* ships, each having lived through a different version of history. These infinite realities reveal that the choices we don't make don't simply go unlived, but that they all play out in alternate universes as real as our own. To restore linear order to space and time, the crew must close the fissure, sending every ship back to its own reality, even if that means back into war or certain death.

I instinctively understood the sci-fi grammar of the show, the critical rupture of no longer being contained by the laws of time and space, and the horror of seeing your every unchosen path laid before you. As an adoptee, I have always felt shadowed by parallel lives: the one where I stay with my birth mother, the one where I am adopted by biological relatives in Taiwan, the ones where I am adopted by families other than mine. I can feel these lives running alongside mine, just as possible and just as real.

I remembered this episode when I received my two birth certificates before I moved out of state and out of my parents' home for the last time after college. I held these beginnings of two versions of my life. My first certificate, issued in Taiwan, holds the Chinese name I was given by my birth mother, who knew me for a day. It lists her name but there is a blank above the line for father. It also records my weight in kilograms and a time of birth sixteen hours ahead of Los Angeles, where my adoptive parents waited for my arrival. There is the original Chinese version and an English translation of that first certificate. After my adoption was finalized, I was issued an American certificate titled "Court Order Delayed Registration of Birth." It contained my new English first, middle, and last name and my adoptive parents' names as mother and father. The American document contains all the correct details about my birth in Taiwan. It is dated January 1983, when I was a year and a half old.

By the time I was born, my parents had struggled with infertility for all thirteen years of their marriage, their pain sharpened by stigma, their siblings' growing families, and fears of invasive treatments. I always knew that I was adopted, so they must have explained it to me when I was very young. I never had a sit-down-we-have-something-to-tell-you moment. But I also knew never to ask questions. "You don't *feel* adopted," my mom once said to me. "I *feel* like you grew in my stomach." It was her way of saying she didn't love me any differently than she would a biological child. What I heard was that being adopted was something she could overcome with her love. Once, maybe around age eight, I said wanted to meet my birth mom someday, that I wanted to know where I came from and who I'm related to. I had been curious for years, but this was the first time I had ever spoken it aloud. My mom grew somber and carefully explained to me that since I had no idea whether my birth mom had gotten married or had other children, that we couldn't know if my contacting her would come as an unwelcome disruption. "She might have a good life now," my mom said. Her caution sat heavily with me. I began to doubt that my birth mom longed to meet me, as I had always fantasized, and wondered if she was as desperate as my adopted mom to hide the circumstance of my birth. I didn't want to ruin her life a second time.

My mom once told me she and my dad were matched with another infant girl before me. She didn't tell me why that adoption fell through, but she takes it as evidence that I was meant to be her daughter. I didn't share my mom's assurance about how things had worked out. I never wanted to be destined to be separated from my birth mother. Perhaps we all arrive at every moment of our lives by a series of near misses, but the knowledge of this other girl haunted me. I could feel her living a version of my life, which has always felt like a version of infinite other lives, each hinging on the smallest of shifts.

It's easier to talk about adoption in terms of fate and destiny, of being wanted and chosen. As if adoption were not born out of a series of desperate and agonizing choices, some less free than others, which lead to our losses and gains. Adoption is a series of paradoxes: the strangers who form an immediate family; the life given and given up; the two childless mothers of the same daughter. I know the other infant girl and I cannot both be my parents' daughter. Neither can I belong to both my parents and my birth mother. And yet I do.

In the photos of my parents and me meeting for the first time under glaring LAX terminal lights, their faces look young to me, but they said they felt old to be new parents—my mom was thirty-five and my dad forty-two. They had just celebrated their fourteenth wedding anniversary. In the pictures, I am asleep but upright in my mom's arms. My jacket hood is pulled over my head, and my face clutches at sleep. My mom's smile is small and nervous. At just under five feet tall, she looks like she is bearing up a much bigger weight than a nine-month-old. She is bracing me with her whole lower body, like she is going into a weightlifter's squat. My dad is standing beside us, his head tilted toward me with curiosity. I think about my parents becoming parents at that moment, even though my adoption had been arranged before I was born. My aunt's friend, who must have known of my parents' struggle to have a baby, worked as an international Nestlé sales representative, traveling to maternity wards with offers of free powdered milk samples for mothers and babies. At one hospital near Taipei, she met a pregnant teen. After one conversation, my aunt's friend contacted my parents and brought the girl to an agency that would handle the adoption. My parents would ask her to be my godmother, a nonreligious Chinese honorific.

After all those years of working in the restaurant together, I wonder what my mom said to my Auntie Betty about wanting children, and what my Auntie Betty said to her friend that made her leap to make such arrangements with a girl she had just met. I wonder what the years were like when Auntie Betty's daughter and two sons were born, my mom helping to care for them while cooking for customers and yearning. I wonder how my parents waited for nine months while my adoption and immigration paperwork were processed, receiving occasional pictures of me in a foster home with caregivers and other children. Those first months must have felt stolen from them, my life in Taiwan torturously parallel to theirs.

When I finally arrived in Los Angeles, I belonged to them alone, and their lives as parents could begin. But my life was already underway, my ear attuned to Taiwanese Mandarin, my senses tied to that foster home. I know now from watching both my daughters how much a nine-month-old understands, how much they can say, ask for, recognize, and know. At that age, my girls pointed to the fridge when they were hungry, came charging into the bathroom when they heard the tub starting to fill, picked their favorite books at bedtime, and reached for the person they wanted to hold them. But belonging to my parents meant amputating that first portion of my life, those first nine months of their waiting and my becoming myself without them. My second birth certificate marks the beginning of my life with them and the end of another they would never talk about.

There were few things I hated more than visiting my godmother. I saw her once a year when she stopped by my aunt's house on her visits to the United States. Her three grown children all lived in different states, and she split her time between their homes and Taiwan. When my aunt called to say she had arrived, my mom and I would gather bags of candies, fruit, nuts, and other gifts for my godmother and walk across the street to Auntie Betty's house. My mom curled her hair and put on makeup and her nicest clothes.

She scrutinized my hair, my outfit, and my face to make sure I was presentable. Paying homage to my godmother for making our lives possible was the one time a year we acknowledged my adoption, yet at no point during these visits did we ever *talk* about it. I sat between my mom and the woman who had brought me to her, and who had met my birth mother, desperately curious but unable to ask a single question. My job was to present myself well, to behave, smile, and show her what a good job I was doing at living the very good life I had been given. My godmother always greeted me warmly but wasn't confident with her English skills, and so never said anything beyond how tall I was getting and asking if I was getting good grades. My mom hardly talked during these visits either. She nursed a mug of tea with her head lowered, and we both mostly listened as my godmother and Auntie Betty caught up with each other in Taiwanese Mandarin. When the visit was over, we walked back home and back into the world where we pretended my adoption wasn't something we ever needed to talk about. The cognitive dissonance of thanking the person who had helped create our family, while those very means of creation were at all other times a shameful secret, was excruciating, and for hours after every visit, I remained agitated and sullen.

I sometimes imagine my parents sitting down to a meal they have waited fourteen years for, starved beyond hunger and unable to believe their agony will finally end. I have never known anything close to such deprivation, but I do know that when my body is aching for food, I cannot savor. My ability to be satiated is ruined. My parents' need for me always felt like a kind of devouring, the space I filled forever throbbing with want. And their protracted grief, never entirely processed or healed, was easily triggered. Anytime I expressed a difficult emotion, adoption related or not, they retreated as if freshly wounded, guarding their broken hearts even from the person who was supposed to be the repair. In the silence around my birth and adoption, I grew ashamed of how I was conceived and born, of not belonging like my cousins did, of not being my parents' first choice in how to build a family. Since I could never be theirs biologically, I became the one who protected them by never mentioning my adoption, never revealing my longing to know my birth family, never being anything but grateful and loyal.

The psychologist Pauline Boss writes that adoption is an ambiguous loss, a kind of loss that "defies closure" and "cannot be resolved." Ambiguous loss occurs when a person is physically present but psychologically absent (as with dementia) or, in reverse, physically absent but psychologically present (a missing person, an adopted child). In both cases, "the status of a loved one as 'there' or 'not there' remain[s] indefinitely unclear." I did not *miss* my birth mother, exactly. But she was, nonetheless, *gone*, and I fantasized about her frequently. I wonder now if a dream life, whether mine with my birth mom or my parents' life with a brood of biological children, can also be a kind of ambiguous loss. Along with adoption, Boss also names immigration as a source of ambiguous loss. My parents had already lost their language, culture, people, and sense of belonging. Perhaps they were already so haunted and pressured to be grateful in the face of dire sacrifice that they could not find a way to share a daughter with her other life.

⁓

The language of initiation into the church is filled with references to adoption. The study guide for the Rite of Christian Initiation of Adults reads, "In the sacrament of Christian initiation . . . we receive the Spirit of filial adoption and we are part of the entire people of God in the celebration of the memorial of the Lord's death and resurrection." Later, the guide states, "Baptism . . . makes us sharers in God's own life and his adopted children." In his letters to the Ephesians, Romans, and Galatians, St. Paul uses the term *huiothesia* to refer to the Roman form of adoption in which an adolescent or grown male comes to live on a family's estate, helps maintain it, and is granted a share of the inheritance in return. *Huios* for "son" and *thesia* for "to place." Entering the family of God resembles this practice of a stranger receiving a place in a home. St. Paul writes that we are all "destined for adoption" by God through Jesus. He adds that none of us are born children and heirs of God; rather, we are all adopted as such: "those who are led by the Spirit of God are the children of God." According to our faith, no one is born a member. Rather, we are all "incorporated into the church" through the ritual of the sacraments. In other words, being a Christian is synonymous with being adopted.

Rather than giving me consolation or making me feel less alone, I found the idea of adoption into the church painful and unsettling. I wanted to feel expectant hope as I moved toward the next step of receiving my sacraments, becoming a catechumen, but I couldn't shake this sense of dread and mourning. The term *catechumen* comes from the Greek *katēchein*, which means "echoing down" and shares its root with *catechism*, which means "teaching by word of mouth." One becomes a catechumen during the Rite of Acceptance and makes a public declaration of one's desire and decision to receive instruction, the sacraments, and acceptance into the church. I wanted to join the church family, but I did not want to be adopted by God. The idea was too fraught. I didn't even like the Scripture metaphors of God as a parent—a nursing mother or forgiving father—even if God was protective, merciful, and comforting. My own adoption felt like an appendage deprived of blood supply that had become withered and numb.

And yet, I needed to move forward with my initiation. I felt more pulled than pursuant. My commitment had been set in motion, and while following through felt at times like a matter of overcoming my hesitations and not quitting this far in, it was more a whole-body hunger I could not quiet. I certainly wanted the parish community, the liturgy, the orientation toward the transcendent, the container large enough for all our gratitude, hopes, obligations, and doubts. But who did I want it for? Not myself severed from my beginnings, pruned of any reminders that I arrived through a series of heartbreaks and griefs, both of which are partners, not inhibitors, to joy. There was just no getting around it. To ask for initiation into the church was to ask for adoption. If I wanted to be baptized, my full self would have to ask to belong.

After my daughters were born, I had begun to believe such re-demption could be possible. My husband and I built our family biologically. My two pregnancies came relatively easily and both girls were full term and healthy. Our choice was not a response to my adoption, but it was not entirely free from it either. Everything I'd ever done, from dating to graduating college and now conceiving my children, was measured against how far it stretched beyond my mom's experience, the distance a measure of my gratitude and guilt.

My daughters each resemble me in different ways. My eldest has my hair texture, my eye color, the shape of my face. My youngest has my hands and feet, lips, dimples, and chin. Both have inherited expressions from me, too—the way we lock our jaws when we're angry, the staccato of our laugh when caught off guard. It's thrilling to see myself in them and to see them when I look in a mirror. Our resemblance was part of our bond, and it amazed me endlessly. Paul, who has been told all his life how strongly he resembles his mother and her family, is no less thrilled by what he shares with the girls—our youngest's eye and hair color, our eldest's smile and curls.

Until I became a parent, I had never known anyone related to me, let alone noticeably so. To my parents, my biology had always been a betrayal. The features that matched neither my mom nor dad—my bridgeless nose, flat cheekbones, larger bone structure—all pointed to the stranger in me, to her visible claim. My mom used to seize upon any ways in which I took after her or my dad—I was tall like him, my handwriting swooped like hers, I tanned in the summer like him. While she mentioned them often, the resemblances always felt like a stretch, a list of mostly coincidental similarities. In truth, I do not look like either of my parents, my features round where my mom's are angular, their composition narrow while my dad's are broad.

Having my daughters transformed my relationship to the features that once separated me from my parents. I was forced to reconcile a paradox: that my girls were beautiful *and* unmistakably carried parts of myself that I had wanted to erase or alter. That I could not love their perfect faces while regretting my own. My daughters relish our alikeness, how, when my eldest wears my clothes, she gets mistaken for me from afar, and when my youngest is sitting with her face touching mine, people do a double take. Very slowly, I've begun welcoming back my features. I've willed myself to love the source of our resemblance.

My parents were thrilled to become grandparents, and they immediately switched from calling and referring to each other as Mommy and Daddy to Grandma and Grandpa. Somewhat surprisingly, they suddenly loved seeing my features that lived in their granddaughters. "This one has your nose, exactly!" my mom would exclaim. "This one has your long legs," she would note. That any of my girls' features might also belong to my birth mother or father was of no concern. My looks, once a threat and a gulf, were now safe to be seen and remarked upon, taken as a source of my daughters' beauty. My parents' newfound comfort with my appearance was something I had often hoped for, yet when it came it was not a relief. It was not a welcoming home for these parts of myself because my parents were no more able to talk about my adoption than before. A barrier to belonging still stood between us. If anything, their shift revealed that it was not them I needed in order to feel seen or restored.

⁓

On the morning of my Rite of Acceptance, there was no announcement of the ceremony to the parish, and I worried over the confusion or impatience parishioners might feel at the delayed start of Mass. I stood in a gray, A-line dress near the altar railing with my husband and our daughters, while Fr. P conducted the ceremony. I held tight to my thrashing two-year-old, who was determined to get to our regular pew and break out her snacks. I had turned thirty-five two days before. I had memorized the script over the weekend and was ready when Fr. P asked me to state my name. Then he asked, "What do you ask of God's church?"

"Faith," I responded.

"What does faith offer you?" he continued.

"Eternal life."

Questions followed about whether I was ready for this phase of my initiation. "Are you prepared to begin this journey today under the guidance of Christ? Are you ready, with the help of God, to live this life? Are you ready to accept these teachings of the Gospel?"

To each I responded, "I am."

Turning to Paul, Fr. P asked if he was ready, as my sponsor, to help me find and follow Christ.

"I am," he replied, steadying our four-year-old by the shoulders as she bounced and swayed.

Then Paul was asked to make the sign of the cross for each of my senses. He moved in front of me and I met his eyes briefly before lowering my gaze to his shoes, bracing myself for the intimacy of his touch in front of onlookers. He signed my ears to hear the word of God, my lips to respond to the word, my heart where Christ will dwell, my shoulders to bear the (gentle) yoke of Christ, my hands to do the work of Christ, the tops of my sandaled feet so that I might walk in the way of Christ. Fr. P said a short prayer, and we moved into the regular liturgy of the Mass, with a few extra catechumen blessings at the end.

Afterward, over coffee and doughnuts that were offered in the basement every Sunday after Mass, people asked me about the ceremony and admitted that they, as lifelong Catholics, had neither seen nor heard of it before. None of them had ever seen an adult receive their first sacraments. They also said my dress was lovely and my children had been well behaved. I refilled all our chipped Boy Scout mugs with tepid coffee, happy to be part of this community and more at ease with the public nature of my initiation. One woman I didn't even know very well reached out and put her hand over mine. "Welcome, dear." She smiled. "Be sure to let me know when you get baptized. I'll want to watch that."

⁓

As soon as I became a catechumen, I began attending weekly meetings with Fr. P to prepare for baptism. The first week, I was asked to choose my confirmation name. Fr. P advised that I select the name of a saint whom I wished to serve as guide, model, and patron. I chose Anne, the mother of Mary, thinking of the blessings of my own motherhood. We also talked through skipping the next step most catechumens take, the Rite of Election, which is the church's formal affirmation of the catechumen's readiness for the sacraments of initiation. Catechumens become "the elect" by gathering at the Cathedral Basilica of St. Louis, formally affirming their desire to join the church, receiving affirmation from their sponsors, and inscribing their names in the Book of the Elect. In St. Louis, the ceremony is only held on the first Sunday of Lent, for those on schedule to be baptized at Easter, so I would simply remain a catechumen until my baptism. The date for which I couldn't seem to nail down.

Our meetings in the rectory conference room had no program or agenda. At our second and third meetings, I read a piece of theology or portions of the *Catholic Catechism for Adults* and brought it in to discuss. I made my way through the entire catechism, some Paul Tillich, Joan Chittister, more Ronald Rolheiser, and Elizabeth A. Johnson, and brought in whatever topics were on my mind that week. We talked mainly about different writers, different eras in church history, and the evolution of church teaching. Fr. P didn't assign me any readings or tasks, and I realized I had no idea when these meetings would end or what we were working toward.

At the end of our fourth meeting, in August, I asked, "Can we talk about my baptism?" We'd spent the meeting talking about more writers and the different ways the Catechism of Christian Doctrine has changed through the centuries. As usual, I mostly led the discussion with what I was reading and the questions that arose. Fr. P listened and offered thoughts and clarifications. But he was running to another meeting and replied, "Let's meet next time, and discuss then."

At our fifth meeting, I asked more explicitly. "Can we set a date for my baptism?"

"You feel ready for baptism?" Fr. P asked.

"Yes," I replied, wondering how that could have been unclear.

"Often," he began, "people are eager to receive their sacrament. But I find it's best to wait and discern. There's no rush."

"No, I guess there's no rush," I admitted. We ended the meeting.

"See you next week," he called as we parted.

I was at a loss about why I couldn't move forward, why we couldn't even have a conversation about receiving the sacraments. I couldn't figure out why he was avoiding the topic, or what I was missing or needed to be doing differently. I was now deeply unsure of whether I was doing *anything* right.

"I know these aren't formal sessions," I said to Paul, trying to figure out what I was missing. "But I actually have no idea what these meetings are for and what I'm supposed to be doing. Am I supposed to be learning something to prepare for baptism? I haven't been asked to."

"I think he owes you an explanation," Paul said. "If he's not being clear about what he wants you to do, then you should ask him."

I knew that at any time over the last five weeks, I could have asked Fr. P what I should be doing now that I was no longer following the RCIA program. I actually liked that I didn't have to wait until Easter or follow a rigid calendar, but I needed *something* to guide me. I hadn't asked because I had been too strangled by resentment: After proclaiming my desire for baptism in front of the entire parish and taking the first steps toward initiation, was I now going to have to beg for or demand it? These meetings had been Fr. P's idea, his request, but he'd offered no structure or expectations. I felt at sea, unguided, and seized with an old terror of moving uncertainly and unprepared through the world.

I arrived at our meeting in September determined not to leave without a baptism date. I didn't wait until the end of the hour to bring it up.

"It's something we should talk more about," Fr. P said. "Let's meet again and revisit."

"No," I refused. "I don't want to do that."

I took Fr. P's nonanswer for the answer it was. I would have happily answered any question or studied any topic, but I had been given no instruction or even advice. I was no longer willing to fumble for an answer when no question had ever been posed. The uncertainty was too much to bear. I would no longer subject myself to these endless meetings and unexplained delays, not even for the sacraments. In that moment, it was all or nothing for me. I wasn't considering a different parish, priest, or path. I was ready to walk away. *If this door isn't going to open*, I thought, *I can stop now*.

I prepared myself to just walk out. But the words came first. "Look, I don't know what it is you want me to say. I'll just tell you that I don't want to get baptized so that I can have faith. It's like, I didn't marry Paul because I was hoping to fall in love *afterward*. That had already happened." My voice rose and shook a little as I continued. "We come here because we like the way our lives have changed, and it feels like everything has changed. Everything feels bigger and fuller, but also . . . I don't even know how to describe it. It all feels *closer*. I feel like the envy and resentment I battle constantly are easier to quiet. Also, we just went out to dinner last night with a guy who showed up to the church and asked us to go to dinner with him. It was very awkward but very lovely, and we're going to do it again next week because that's just what we do now, all this stuff which we never would have done before." I paused, my chest heaving. "I don't know what else you want me to say."

I was flooded with adrenaline, prepared for a fight. But when I finished, Fr. P sighed and lifted his clasped wrists to rest on top of his head, his arms jutted out in the easy posture of someone with a deal about to close his way.

"This," he said, "is the conversation I have been hoping we would have someday." Then he opened his phone's calendar. "I think Sunday, November 20, would be a nice day for a baptism. It's the Solemnity of Christ the King."

"It's what?" I gaped.

He put down his ancient and battered phone. "This conversation—about the movement of God in your life, about why and how you're becoming a Christian—this is what I was hoping all along we would be able to talk about." He smiled. "Thank you."

I learned the word *shibboleth* back in college, from an episode of *The West Wing* in which a persecuted Chinese Christian minister begs the president for asylum, then proves his faith and worthiness of aid by naming Jesus's twelve disciples and saying the word *shibboleth*, all in English. In the book of Judges, *shibboleth* is a password whose pronunciation reveals which tribe a person belongs to, and therefore determines whether they should live or die. The word was an admission of one's loyalty and belonging. With Fr. P, I had felt tested, left to flail for the right answer out of any number of possibilities. I happened to land on the one Fr. P wanted, but what if I had spoken differently? What if I had said the word slightly off?

I went home stunned and indignant. Within twenty minutes, I had gone from bewilderment and nearly abandoning my own conversion to racing toward baptism, when all along, I could have put down the books. I could have avoided feeling lost and confrontational. I could have been baptized months ago.

"I feel like I've been set up," I said to Paul as soon as I got home. "Why didn't he just ask me to tell him how my life has changed?"

"I don't know," he replied. "That seems like an unfair test." After a moment, he continued thoughtfully, "Maybe, in his mind, he didn't feel like he could ask."

"Why would he think that?"

"The only thing I can think of is that asking the question would make it somehow like he was prompting you in one direction, like he was setting you up to pass a test instead of coming up with the answer on your own. Look, I'm not saying it wasn't a really bad way for him to handle it. I'm just guessing at why he might have done it like that."

"Maybe," I sighed.

Maybe my self-imposed reading agenda hadn't left room for me to talk about my own spiritual formation. Maybe I came across like I was striving to understand books more than myself. But how was I to know? I felt an old stirring of anxiety at being left to my own trial and error. At being expected to know without being told. But this was different. My pastor was not my immigrant parents unsteadily navigating a new world. He wasn't depending on me to know the answer because he himself did not. With the power he held over my receiving the sacraments, he could have helped me see, without leading or giving away any answers, that I had been asking the wrong questions.

"Do you want to still get baptized here?" Paul asked. "We can always do it somewhere else."

Even after all this, I wanted to receive the sacraments at our parish, where we'd made our home for the past three years, where I felt needed and welcomed. My experience of the church and my decision to stay or find another place to worship didn't come down to one person. My shibboleth had passed, but it mattered more that I had asked for what I wanted, without embarrassment, with even a little fury. Everything I'd said about the changes in my life had been true and had not been to please or assuage or convince anyone. It was sinking in that I was going to be baptized and become a Catholic.

"Yes," I replied. "It's scheduled. I think I might be starting to get excited about it."

"Good," Paul said. "That's great news. Who should we invite?"

"I don't know." I hesitated. "Do we have to invite anyone?"

"It might be nice to celebrate with people. You know my mom would love to come."

"I don't want a party," I said. "But of course, we could invite your mom." He waited, not needing to ask the next question. "I'm not sure about bringing my parents. They get so anxious when we go anywhere, especially church."

My parents were nervous out of their element. I thought about how they only wanted to stay home with the girls instead of coming with us to Mass. How when I said we would like it if they joined us too, they replied, "We don't know what to do in church." And when I offered to walk them through the Order of the Mass, they sighed, "We never had to do all these things at any of your cousins' weddings." During their visits, we settled on skipping Mass or, if we had an obligation to serve or read during the liturgy, my parents went for a long walk and met us afterward.

What I didn't want to say is that it would be easier without them. Managing their anxieties would be more than I could handle while trying to be fully present to my sacraments. They needed so much from me when they were in a new place. To answer their questions, to reassure them, to know where to go and how to find food and how to validate parking, to present everything in manageable chunks to help settle them.

"If they come," I said to Paul, "I don't know if I would be able to be fully present to what's going on."

"I get it," he replied. "We can do whatever works. I'm so happy for you."

～

According to the Rite of Christian Initiation of Adults, my period as a catechumen was complete. Next were the three Scrutinies. These rites are celebrated during Mass in the weeks leading up to baptism, "in order to deliver the elect from the power of sin and Satan, to protect them against temptation, and to give them strength in Christ." Part of the spiritual purification that usually happens during Lent, the Scrutinies also involve exorcism.

"Don't sweat the Scrutinies," Sr. V wrote in an email. "It's a terrible word."

I knew Sr. V wouldn't be able to make it to my baptism. She'd only been settled in her new job for two months. But I wanted her to know that I had a date for my baptism.

The exorcisms, I was glad to discover, weren't about driving out Satan the way we see in movies. They were instead designed to inspire "a desire for purification and redemption by Christ" and present me formally with the Creed and the Lord's Prayer, "the ancient texts that have always been regarded as expressing the heart of the Church's faith and prayer."

While there were supposed to be three Scrutinies, the date of my baptism was approaching so fast that Fr. P said we would be fine with just two. The looseness of the schedule was a relief. But I did wonder if there would have been time had I not spent five weeks attending uncertain meetings with Fr. P.

During my second Scrutiny, only one week before my baptism, the exorcism portion was thankfully brief. Before the regular liturgy began, I stood facing the altar, Fr. P at my right with his hand on my shoulder. He asked God to free me from false values and lies, and asked Jesus to stir my desire for good, light, and fearless witness. I returned to my family in our pew until after the homily, when I was called to kneel before the altar. In front of the seated congregation, I was instructed to pray silently for the freedom to be a child of God. The others were invited to pray for me. Then, while I remained kneeling, everyone behind me stood for the prayers of intercession, responding, "Lord, hear our prayer," after the priest read each one. I felt exposed before all the people staring at my back, which was aching along with my knees and shinbones.

But after the second or third prayer and response, my attention turned to the uneven hems of the altar cloths, to Jesus's muted expression on the crucifix hanging behind the altar, and the tiny kneelers for altar servers that I had never noticed before. As we all responded in unison, I relaxed a little until, in his concluding the prayer, Fr. P said, "Hear our prayers for Melody, whom you have called to be your adopted daughter."

I returned to my seat shaken and edgy. The words seared me, magnifying my exposure. I was grateful to stay seated for the rest of Mass and waited for the rhythms of the liturgy to settle my agitation. I remembered that when I was in sixth grade, my best friend, whom I had known half my life, found out that I was adopted. She had asked about my birthplace, and I had replied, "Taiwan," without thinking. "Were your parents, like, on vacation or something?" she had asked, giggling. I told her the truth, hesitantly. It was a relief that someone knew at last. I asked her not to tell anyone, and she wrapped her pinky around mine to seal her promise. The next day my friend mentioned, innocently, that her mom had been surprised to learn this about me. She was stunned by my shock and anger. "I only told my mom. I tell her everything!" she cried. I clutched my stomach, unable to move or breathe. My core seemed to collapse. I couldn't stand up straight. I only realized in adulthood that what I'd experienced was a panic attack. Unable to get me to the lunch line, my teacher sent me to the nurse. I pretended to have cramps and lay doubled over on the vinyl cot all afternoon, on the brink of vomiting, every part of me flayed open, raw and pulsing at my betrayal of my parents. Though they had never expressly forbidden me from telling anyone, I knew, as surely as I knew our phone number, that I should never talk about my adoption. I had carried it all this time, never as my own story but as a secret I kept for them.

But for my family and a few good friends, no one in the church with me that morning had any idea that I was adopted. But they had all prayed for me to hear and answer the call to be an adopted daughter. Their intercession held me together. Within their collective desire and hope for me, my adoption shifted into something that I could hold private but not in secret. As a convert, adoption was a sacred obligation I'd been given to fulfill, without any shame or fear of being exposed. As a fact of my life, maybe adoption could be simply something that was mine to share or not. It did not have to be locked into regret or disappointment. In my pew, among my family, I checked to make sure I could feel all my extremities. I was still there, still intact. My urge to flee from danger had subsided, washed into the notes of the Communion hymn. I was not free from my difficult relationship with adoption, and my entering the church would not alter or supersede my first adoption. But neither did my two adoptions need to define or limit each other. Maybe my second adoption could resurrect some of the first one's losses. I began to hope for what an adult adoption might offer: a place for me with room for the life to come and the life already lived.

〜

I received three sacraments of initiation—baptism, Eucharist, and confirmation—on a November Sunday at our parish. I wore a soft white sweater for my baptismal garment. My family and I sat in the front row, something we'd never done before. The novelty and proximity to the action kept my daughters entertained and almost still throughout Mass. That day's liturgy remains something of a blur and I have only a few pictures of the ceremony, but I remember the stained glass on the south side of the building blazed bright at 10:00 a.m., the marble font standing with its heavy top ajar, and the pews feeling fuller than usual. The church was warm against the blustery day.

To be baptized, I was called forth to receive a blessing, then my family was called to join me by the font. I remember Fr. P telling me to expect a lot of water. "It has to be flowing," he said, as if it wouldn't count otherwise. When I leaned over the font, I wish I could say I was deep in prayer or entranced by the Holy Spirit. Mostly, I was hoping my sweater didn't ride up in the back and that I didn't pitch forward into the thick, bone-shattering marble. The freezing holy water really did gush at all three pours—in the name of the Father, Son, and Holy Spirit—soaking the top of my head and cascading down my neck. I stood, dripping, while Fr. P lit my baptismal candle and handed it to Paul, my sponsor, instructing him to keep the light of Christ with me. I dripped while Fr. P drew a sign of the cross on my forehead with the earthy chrism oil. I dripped all the way back to my seat, where my three-year-old retracted her outstretched arms when she got a look at me. She gaped incredulously at the state of my hair and clothes, which would have earned her, at the very least, a time-out. Shaking her head, she whispered, "Look at you! You spilled!"

After the liturgy of the Eucharist, Fr. P called me up to the altar. I stood facing the marble slab and held out my hands. In them, he placed a shard of altar bread, which was a wafer as big as a tea saucer, held up during the transformation of bread into the Body of Christ, then cracked into small pieces and mixed with the perfectly round wafers for Communion. The sharp edges bristled my cheek. I reached across the wide altar to receive the wine, which perfumed my throat just as it did when I received Communion months before in New Mexico. My mouth still full of the Body and

Blood, I stepped over to receive my confirmation. It's a strange and compressed sequence of sacraments for adult converts, as confirmation is usually received around age thirteen, six years after your first Communion. The sacrament is supposed to renew your infant baptism and confirm your adult commitment to the faith. Again, I was anointed with chrism and the priest's words, "Be sealed with the gift of the Holy Spirit."

I returned to my pew and settled onto the kneeler as the other parishioners were invited up to receive Communion as usual. With my face behind my folded hands, I watched the crowd in what I used to see as an uncomfortable parade. I used to anticipate feeling embarrassed to be in the line, on display and making a show of the sacrament. But their movements felt different that day, everyone finding their place in the aisles, holding up the line to let people dart back to their seats, coming to receive just as Jesus had instructed. The Gospels contain many more parables and elliptical lessons than direct instructions, but this part is explicit: "Do this in memory of me." Filing back to their seats, some parishioners paused before me in the front pew, rolling the Body of Christ to one side of their mouths to smile at me and my family. Some laid their hands over mine or on my wet shoulder. Some touched my sodden hair.

As the Communion meditation song began and the undistributed Communion hosts were tucked into the tabernacle, we all heaved up from the kneelers and sat back down. I thought, *Next week, I'll do this all over again.* My first sacraments were not the culmination of my conversion, but the introduction of regular and ordinary holiness. It was like being shown what breakfast is for the first time and told that it would be available daily if I wanted it. I only needed to arrive hungry.

In the end, I didn't invite my parents to the ceremony. I had perfectly good reasons: they would feel anxious, confused, and alone while my family was absorbed in the ceremony. My parents know that church is part of my life and are content and accepting, but faith isn't a topic we enter together. Church is not a space they are comfortable sharing with me. Maybe I also wanted to spare them watching me be received into another family, from viewing but not participating in yet another initiation of mine. I hoped this one would not separate us further but might someday give me ways to approach, however gradually, reconciliation. In becoming Catholic, I would not leave my parents behind, but I could stop waiting for them. A Chinese daughter stays near her parents in both proximity and service. Duty demands that she walks with them as a guide and support, going only as fast as they go, and only as far. They could not come with me into this part of life, in which I discovered all that I must grieve, and in which I gained a language for how to live, a vocabulary for the divine, for our common humanity, for reconciliation and holy desires. But I could go.

In the swelling harmonies of the song "How Excellent Is Thy Name," newly baptized and confirmed, I heard God say *yes*. Prayer always comes upon me like this. I hear God's answer before I even know my own question. What I wanted to know was whether everything I had brought with me was okay. I was not just asking about sins and forgiveness, but about everything hidden, rejected, lost. Everything still waiting to be called back home. All the petty and disordered and vicious. Nothing, I was assured in God's answer, as time seemed stretched and stilled and my daughters miraculously kept to their seats, was so far gone as to not be welcome here. I came to faith desiring more. I was being given permission to stop trying to bring less. I could not have come to receive the sacraments severed from any part of myself. I could feel some of them being stitched together as I sat bathed in oil and water.

In Romans 8:22, St. Paul writes, "We know that all creation is groaning in labor pains even until now; and not only that, but we ourselves, who have the firstfruits of the Spirit, we also groan within ourselves as we wait for adoption, the redemption of our bodies." My waiting was not over. It was now joined to my parish family's. For however long we might have until the final adoption, we wait together, as St. Paul says, with endurance.

A few days after my sacraments, my certificate arrived in the mail. It looked something like a participation award—vanilla cardstock with a swooping silver border. On it are my full English name and my confirmation name, Anne, which is the fourth name I have been given in my life, used only once as I was receiving the sacrament of confirmation. There isn't a space for my name given at birth, or my Cantonese name, Fui Ghen, chosen by my paternal grandfather, or for Nui, which means "daughter" in Cantonese and is the only name my parents have ever called me. The name recorded for my baptism is the name I am known by outside my first homes. This is the version of me who feels it has become Catholic, this is who the convert is. But the other parts have turned too, a conversion toward the single self I must now try to piece together in the belief that wholeness is what I am called to, what I am built for.

Looking again, I also saw on the certificate the name of my husband as my sponsor, the date and place of my birth, the names of both my parents, the name of our church, and Fr. P's signature. The space was filled with all these words, reaching all the way to the edges. It could barely contain them all, and yet this was not the whole story. So much was missing and so much was yet to come. I am learning that the divine is all our fleshy bodies, the ones I know to miss and the ones I must imagine. They are here and absent, gone and present. They are intimate and stranger, silent and singing, all of us a communion, carrying what we carry, as far as we can.

MYSTAGOGY

The famous conversion story of Saul appears in chapter 9 of the Acts of the Apostles. Saul of Tarsus, a persecutor "breathing murderous threats" against Jesus's disciples, travels to Damascus on a mission to arrest anyone affiliated with the early Christian community. While on the road, light flashes in the sky and Saul falls to the ground, hearing a voice ask, "Saul, Saul, why are you persecuting me?" Jesus identifies himself as the voice, then tells Saul to go into the city and await instructions. Saul's traveling companions hear the voice too but are astonished to see no one around who could have spoken. When Saul arises, he finds himself blind, and his attendants lead him into Damascus, where he goes without food, water, or sight for three days.

I thought Saul's was a conversion to strive for. Throughout my seeking and sacraments, I wanted an encounter with God so powerful that it would lay me out. I also wanted a bright line between my old and new selves, which in Saul's example is to say, the bad and good selves. My slow, steady conversion did not excite me. It was not flashy. It's not that I wanted a radically different life, but I worried that not enough had changed.

When I reread the account of Saul's conversion recently, I noticed some things I'd never seen before. First, Saul does not fall from a horse or wear a Roman uniform, as much of Western art depicts. Saul is Jewish, and some sources identify him as a member of the priestly class. Also, Saul doesn't hit his head on a rock and concuss himself to faith. He is *already* a man of faith, with authority from the high priest and the synagogues in Damascus to arrest any of Jesus's followers because they have broken with ancient religious laws and customs. In persecuting heresy, Saul is serving God. His conversion, then, is not from nothing into belief. It is rather from one understanding of God's instructions to another, requiring a wholly different expression of his faith and a new orientation for his life and work.

I also realized that it was not the fall on the road but an encounter with the disciple Ananias in Damascus that transformed Saul. At first reluctant to minister to a virulent persecutor of Jesus's followers, Ananias is reassured by God that Saul has been chosen to serve, that God will show Saul "what he will have to suffer for my name," and that God has already given Saul a vision of Ananias restoring his sight. Obediently, Ananias accepts Saul into his home and lays his hands on Saul, calling him "my brother." In that moment, Saul regains his sight, gets up, and gets baptized. It is human touch and compassion that restores. Most interestingly, and contrary to widely popular belief, Saul is *not* renamed Paul after his conversion. He is called Saul until Acts 13, which mentions briefly that he is "also known as Paul." "The use of a double name, one Semitic (Saul), the other Greco-Roman (Paul), is well attested," reads a footnote on the United States Conference of Catholic Bishops website. The dramatic conversion story I had envied did not live up to my imagination. It didn't even live up to its own reputation.

The final phase of initiation into the church is called mystagogy, from the Greek meaning "leading into a mystery." It is a time of formation for the newly baptized to be led from the visible signs of the sacraments into reflecting on and dwelling in the invisible mysteries of faith. In the late fourth century, after the Roman Empire adopted Christianity as its official religion, church leaders felt compelled to help the flood of new converts understand their sacraments by writing commentaries and interpretations. These formative guides were created for those who desired sacraments first and explanations later. Today, the period of mystagogy is sometimes contained within the fifty days between one's sacraments at Easter and the celebration of Pentecost, but is also considered every Christian's lifelong period of formation and quest to understand their sacraments.

After my baptism in November 2016, I reentered regular life abruptly, swept straight into the seasons of Advent and Christmas. Since I never followed a formal RCIA process, I tried to make out for myself where the sacraments might have altered or refined the contours of my life, or not. The first weeks after were aglow with new commitments to prayer, Scripture reading, Mass, and reconciliation (going to confession). Those already regular parts of my life took on a bit of a new thrill and intensity. But in most ways, my life felt the same. Still, I hoped, even suspected, that something visible might yet await. I wanted that flash of light.

What I got was a voice and a *no*.

After seven years of teaching at my city's community college, I was laid off along with twenty of my colleagues, all of us the youngest, least senior, and in all honesty, most enthusiastic faculty. Still a relatively new convert, only one year since I received the sacraments, I thought I might try to pray about it during Advent, having received my pink slip just after Thanksgiving. The layoff was messy and acrimonious. We shouted and hoisted signs at board meetings. We wrote to the papers, to higher education journals, to alderpersons and alumni. I was angry at the governor for shorting the education budget; at the chancellor for only ever using the terms *right-sizing, resource reallocation,* or *reduction in force;* at the faculty union for having agreed to a work contract so vague and full of holes you could sail a cruise ship through it; and at the administration for refusing to even consider cutting other costs to preserve jobs. And I was panicked about my career, my salary, and my purpose in life. After years of adjunct or lecturer positions, I had secured my dream job: a full-time position teaching developmental English at a community college ten minutes from home. I loved the students, who lived in my city, often in my neighborhood, and needed my class to prepare for credit-bearing college writing courses and to dispel the many myths they held about writing and their own worth and abilities. I taught alongside a colleague I admired and with whom I built up the developmental program. This was where I envisioned carrying out my life's work until I retired. Throughout Advent, the pain and betrayal of being laid off was acute. I hadn't even begun to acknowledge my grief.

A few nights before Christmas, I sat up into the early hours by our lighted tree. Numb and reeling, I wanted to pray but couldn't bring myself to approach God with such anger. I didn't want rescue or relief. I just wanted my rage and my wound. Unable to form any of that into prayer, I sat in the winter darkness that matched my insides, the hum of our daughters' white noise machine playing behind me, and sank under the question, *What am I going to do?* The voice was soft but unmistakable, a woman's voice I thought was maybe just my own, but it was too far away and too calm. It didn't ring out from the sky or any corner of the house. It was as much in my head as all around me. *Your instructions have not changed.* I actually glanced around, my heart quickening. I closed my eyes and listened again, but the room, fuller now than it had been a moment ago, was still. The feeling came first, a quiet solidness in my feet on the rug, my body curled into the chair. Then came belief in the voice.

In the weeks following, I still worried. I still drove my anger straight into walls and lashed out through op-eds and social media posts. But the edge had softened. The boat had steadied. I asked my husband if I had probably imagined the whole thing in an anxious fever dream. "I think it was real," Paul replied. "Because 'Your instructions have not changed' sounds absolutely nothing like you. Seriously, who even talks like that? It sounds like more than something you just told yourself." The voice did not cure my layoff grief or my fear, but I was assured that my instructions were larger than my career, that I could sustain the upheaval because the layoff was a major but single event in my life. What I needed to do was go to Mass, be in community, serve, accompany, listen, follow.

There is only one other time I have heard anything like the voice after my layoff. It was during my first mammogram appointment four years later, just after I turned forty. Because I'm adopted, my risk for breast cancer is unknown. My medical history is a blank, and when I go to the doctor I feel very alone with this lack of knowledge. My body feels unanchored, severed from context. I carry unknowns that feel both empty and very heavy. To establish a baseline for my future scans, the radiologist took many images from many angles. They were trying, she explained, to understand what was normal for my tissue so they could spot concerns later. After a doctor reviewed my first images, I was sent back for a second set, only on my left side. After that, they ordered a sonogram. As reassuring as the tech tried to be about how they didn't know anything for certain yet, my stomach cramped and my breath shuddered. I waited, my gown half untied and my chest feeling mangled, in a mauve room with several vases of flowers and boxes of tissues. I had absolutely no information to act upon, yet whatever was inside me was already there or not. Paul was solemn and reassuring on the phone. "Either you're in the clear, or they've caught something really early. Those are both good outcomes."

The sonogram flashed grainy amoebas of my tissue on the same screen that had made my heart leap during pregnancy checkups. But these images were only black teardrops outlined in bright white. I watched the screen, afraid to breathe. The tech began retracing the same strip of skin a dozen times, angling around one bulbous black area, and I began to cry silently. She saved image after image, her eyes trained hard on the screen, the gelled wand probing and stopping, probing and stopping.

I wanted to pray but was bereft of words. I said a flat Our Father and a Hail Mary just to put something on my lips. I catastrophized into a future of wrestling death with chemo and surgery. I refused the possibility of leaving Paul and our girls. I had absolutely no interest in a valiant fight. There was too much left for us to do, too much time we needed and deserved, to even entertain the thought. The whole idea of dying was enraging, unthinkable, and utterly unjust.

As the tech left to find a doctor to review the sonogram images, a plea formed on my tongue. That God make it so my scans were negative. That God not let cancer be inside me. Something stopped me from finishing, pushing the request back. It was in the exact way that I stop my daughter approaching me with her empty dessert bowl, the way I put up my hand and cut her off with, "Do not even ask me for seconds." There was a hand, practically in my face, telling me to stop right there, that mine was the absolute wrong question. My saying it would mean I, and not others, deserved to be cancer free. That I, and not others, had too much to live for and too little time to waste on cancer. That my time ought to be long but not theirs. It would turn God into arbiter and disease assigner. *Okay*, I said. *Fine. I won't ask for that. But I don't want to be here by myself.* The new prayer landed softly and was allowed: *Stay with me, please.* The room echoed with assurance. *Yes, of course. Yes, I will. Yes, I am already.* I wiped my face on my gown and sat up. I was still terrified. I still wanted what I wanted. But I knew that the relationship I sought with God prevented me from asking it of God.

A young resident came in to tell me that they weren't certain I had a mass. Her face was calm and her eyes locked onto mine. It wasn't a negative scan, but anything warranting a biopsy needed to be confirmed as abnormal from two or more angles. For me, they could only capture one angle. Most likely, she said, it was just that my tissue was "heterogeneously dense and asymmetrical." She told me to come in for a follow-up in six months. Relief coursed through me and kept me from feeling much of anything, except a little slimy and lopsided. My body's interior threat neutralized, I came back into space and time. I could feel my extremities once again. I called Paul as I got dressed and heard him exhale as I recounted what happened.

"I cried in front of people," I moaned.

"Maybe focus more on the part where you had an encounter with the divine," he suggested.

I had always imagined such encounters with more grandeur and less reprimand. More comfort instead of correction. When I read the end of Saul's conversion story in Acts 9:20, I realized that his real conversion was not from unbelief to belief, but from certainty to uncertainty. Filled with zeal after his baptism, Saul preaches about Jesus throughout Damascus. The result is hardly glorious. The religious leaders turn on him and plot to execute him, even guarding the city gates against his escape. But his fellow disciples sneak him out through a hole in the city wall and lower him to safety in a basket. From there, he heads to Jerusalem, where disciples who had known him previously reject him, unconvinced that he is no longer a traitorous threat. Again, Saul's preaching stirs the religious to kill him, and he is finally sent away from Jerusalem, back to his homeland, Tarsus. Before conversion, Saul knew who his enemies were and what his duty to his faith was, while the new life he chose exposed him to danger, rejection from all sides, contradiction, and exile. And yet, I believe he wouldn't have given it back for the order and certainty he once knew.

I was drawn to Catholicism because it is a deeply embodied faith—consuming the Body and Blood, the fleshy art and iconography, feast days and fasting days, dripping holy water and chrism, burning candles and incense. These all help me try to comprehend a body's crucifixion, resurrection, and incarnation. Worshipping among others reorients me beyond my little universe and toward the whole of the church. I feel very solid, very real during Mass. I feel part of something very human. Initiation into mystery is ongoing, resistance-filled work to embrace, dwell in, even have gratitude for what is hidden, what I don't understand, and what I can't control. An acquaintance once asked, when I was a very new convert, whether Catholics believe they are consuming the DNA of Jesus when receiving Communion. "No," I replied at the time. I had no words other than, "I don't think it works like that." It took me a long time to learn that were such a thing possible, it would not secure my faith but diminish it, and it would drain the sacred out of our world. We know that Jesus said, "This is my body." We have to live with the mystery of how this can be. My new faith did not grant me a set of beliefs or rules to rely on. It was more like a handrail popping up through dense fog. I still had to make my way as blindly as everyone else, but I was no longer unsteady or on my own.

It's been seven years since I parted ways with teaching. The end came for me, but I still had to release many things—a vocation, part of my identity, my students. I kept to my instructions and slowly could admit that I had been burning out from battling the college administration over every credit hour, dollar, and initiative, and feeling guilty for skipping conferences or stealing class planning time to write. At last, I was able to imagine, after fourteen years in the only career I had ever known, making a go at freelance writing in early 2018, when remote work was already more popular than I could have imagined. My new career came with a lot of false starts, bad gigs, ignorance, naivete, and anxiety, but the change was, overall, a good one, and the benefits to my time, energy, flexibility, and income were inarguable. Still, freelancing is uncertain. This terrified me at first, and so I took on every low-paying or ill-fitting job that came my way, in much the same way that I signed up for every Bible study, spiritual retreat, and daily prayer email when I first began seeking. The first time I lost a freelance job was when a particularly difficult client abruptly terminated our work midcontract. What should have been a three-week job had dragged into a fourth month of tense collaborations, with routine rejections of my work, surreal additions to the realistic novel I was supposed to be ghostwriting, and complaints about my fee. I longed to walk away but was too afraid to lose the income. When I opened the client's email and read that she no longer needed my services, I leaped out of my chair. I was never so happy to be fired, even if it meant not knowing what job would come next. I've had many contracts cut short or drag out because clients change their minds, get transferred, or get their budgets cut. I could roughly plan my work and income month by month. But I've realized that clinging to something narrows my vision. With teaching and the difficult client, I was unable to imagine a different way. I could not have conceived of the blessing of becoming more present, more available, because of a *no*. Years after my conversion, I am finally beginning to live with the uncertainties that have always been there.

The physician Rachel Naomi Remen writes, "When we pray, we stop trying to control life and remember that we belong to life." For as long as I can remember, I have wanted life to be more than just a path we steer away from danger and death, more than just a time we struggle to extend against the odds and against our limitations. I have wanted to belong to life, to its endeavors and its risks, to myself and others, to the ecstasy and ruin that lurk beneath everything worthwhile. To belong to life, I must let myself be carried by it, I must pray, and I must love the end as much as any part of the rest. In the Nicene Creed, we declare our belief in the "maker of heaven and earth, of all things visible and invisible." I say these words aloud with everyone at every Mass, attesting to my belief that the one who made me is also the one who made all things invisible, and who made *the* invisible. I belong to that life as well, which sometimes feels as material as the one I occupy now, filled with saints and ancestors, the Holy Spirit, light and shadow. I am standing inside both, turning, always, toward.

ACKNOWLEDGMENTS

I give grateful acknowledgment to the magazines and journals that first published parts of the following essays in this collection. Parts of "Idiolect" appeared as "Language and Conversion" in *Commonweal* magazine. Parts of "Chinese American" appeared as "Jack's Kitchen" in *Copper Nickel*. Parts of "Pretty Liturgies" appeared as "We Carry Smoke and Paper" in *Blood Orange Review*. Parts of "Invitations" appeared as "Why I Came, Why I Stay" in *Commonweal* magazine. Parts of "Luck Let Go" appeared in *Barnstorm Journal*. Parts of "Redemption Story" appeared as "Back Home" in *North Dakota Quarterly*. Parts of "Two Adoptions" appeared in *Commonweal* magazine. Parts of "Mystagogy" appeared as "After Our Roots Have Thirsted" in *Essay Daily*.

Thank you to the editors of *Commonweal* magazine, especially Kate Lucky and Katie Daniels, for your peerless editing of the three essays that grew into this book.

Thank you to the Regional Arts Commission of St. Louis and the Sustainable Arts Foundation for their funding and support of this book's early writing, and their unmatched dedication to the arts and parents.

Thank you to the places that provided me with the time, beauty, food, and fellowship I needed to create: Kundiman, The Writer's Colony at Dairy Hollow, the Fireplace, the White House Jesuit Retreat, and the Mercy Conference and Retreat Center.

Thank you to my nonfiction professor, Gregory Martin, for teaching me about craft and hard work.

Thank you to my spiritual director, Virginia Herbers, whose patience, openness, humor, and grace made faith possible for me.

Thank you to Jonathan Sawday for reading this book with care and offering great wisdom, wit, and much-needed questions.

Thank you to Michaella A. Thornton for your compassion, humor, tenderness, coffee dates, and unabashed cheerleading and love.

Thank you to Anna Agniel for your feedback, laughter, generosity, and friendship, and for believing in this book from the beginning.

Thank you to Charlie Sidebottom at Vincent's Jewelers in Creve Coeur, Missouri, for your patience and honesty.

Thank you to all my families, to which I am grateful to belong. Thank you to my birth family. Thank you to my family of origin, Jack and Linda Gee, and all the Gees, Lees, Fongs, Kwans, and SooHoos. Thank you to my family of marriage: the Lynchs, Wards, Resnicks, and Waldrons. Thank you to my faith family at St. Pius V in St. Louis.

Thank you to my daughters for my every joy, invitation, and delight.

Thank you to my husband, Paul. You are my faith, my home, and my truest belonging.

BIBLIOGRAPHY

Aristotle. *Aristotle's Poetics*. New York: Hill and Wang, 1961.

Boss, Pauline. *Ambiguous Loss: Learning to Live with Unresolved Grief*. Cambridge, MA: Harvard University Press, 1999.

Boyle, Gregory. "The Calling of Delight: Gangs, Service, and Kinship." Interview by Krista Tippett. *On Being with Krista Tippett*, February 26, 2013. https://onbeing.org/programs/greg-boyle-the-calling-of-delight-gangs-service-and-kinship/.

———. *Tattoos on the Heart: The Power of Boundless Compassion*. New York: Simon and Schuster, 2010.

Chang, Iris. *The Chinese in America: A Narrative History*. New York: Penguin, 2004.

Galadza, Daniel. "The Liturgical Year and Mystagogy." *Logos: A Journal of Eastern Christian Studies* 59, no. 1–4 (2018): 173–92.

Gottschall, Jonathan. *The Storytelling Animal: How Stories Make Us Human*. Boston: Mariner, 2012.

Haight, Roger. *Spiritual and Religious: Explorations for Seekers*. Maryknoll, NY: Orbis, 2016.

International Committee on English in the Liturgy. *Rite of Christian Initiation of Adults Study Guide*. Chicago: Liturgy Training Publications, 1985.

James, William. *The Varieties of Religious Experience*. New York: Barnes and Noble, 2004.

Lewis, C. S. *The Screwtape Letters: Letters from a Senior to a Junior Devil*. New York: Harper Collins, 1998.

Meade, Michael. *The Water of Life: Initiation and the Tempting of the Soul*. Seattle: Greenfire Press, 2006.

Norris, Kathleen. *Amazing Grace: A Vocabulary of Faith*. New York: Riverhead, 1998.

Nouwen, Henri. *Life of the Beloved: Spiritual Living in a Secular World*. New York: Crossroads, 2002.

O'Brien, Kevin. "Ignatian Contemplation and Imaginative Prayer." In *The Ignatian Adventure: Experiencing the Spiritual Exercises of St. Ignatius in Daily Life*. Chicago: Loyola Press, 2011. https://www.ignatianspirituality.com/ignatian-prayer /the-spiritual-exercises/ignatian-contemplation-imaginative -prayer/.

Ó Tuama, Pádraig. "The Fantastic Argument of Being Alive." Interview by Krista Tippet. *On Being with Krista Tippett*, March 2, 2017. https://onbeing.org/programs/padraig -o-tuama-this-fantastic-argument-of-being-alive/.

Remen, Rachel Naomi. *My Grandfather's Blessings: Stories of Strength, Refuge, and Belonging*. New York: Riverhead, 2000.

Rodriguez, Richard. *Hunger of Memory: The Education of Richard Rodriguez*. New York: Bantam, 1982.

Rohr, Richard. "The Circle Dance of God." Center for Action and Contemplation, March 16, 2022. https://cac.org/daily -meditations/the-circle-dance-of-god-2022-03-16/.

Rolheiser, Ronald. *Prayer: Our Deepest Longing*. Cincinnati: Franciscan Media, 2013.

———. *Sacred Fire: A Vision for a Deeper Human and Christian Maturity*. New York: Image, 2014.

Smith, James K. A. *Desiring the Kingdom: Worship, Worldview, and Cultural Formation*. Grand Rapids: Baker Academic, 2009.

Takaki, Ronald. *Strangers from a Different Shore*. New York: Back Bay, 1989.

Tan, Amy. "An Evening with Amy Tan." Purdue University Libraries' Distinguished Lecture Series, West Lafayette, IN, October 4, 2006.

Teilhard de Chardin, Pierre. "Patient Trust." In *Hearts on Fire: Praying with the Jesuits*, edited by Michael Harter. Chicago: Loyola Press, 2005.

Tetlow, Joseph. *The Spiritual Exercises of Ignatius Loyola*. New York: Crossroads, 2009.

United States Conference of Catholic Bishops. "Acts of the Apostles, Chapter 9." USCCB, n.d. https://bible.usccb.org /bible/acts/9.

―――. "Books of the Bible." USCCB, n.d. https://bible.usccb .org/bible.

―――. United States Catholic Catechism for Adults. Washington, DC: USCCB, 2006.

van der Kolk, Bessel. *The Body Keeps the Score: Brain, Mind, and Body in the Healing of Trauma*. New York: Penguin, 2015.

Wiman, Christian. *My Bright Abyss: Meditation of a Modern Believer*. New York: Farrar, Straus and Giroux, 2013.

Yang, Jisheng. *Tombstone: The Great Chinese Famine, 1958–1962*. New York: Farrar, Straus and Giroux, 2008.